THE NEW FEDERALISM

The question of the relation of the states
to the federal government is the cardinal
question of our constitutional system. . . .
It cannot, indeed, be settled by the opinion
of any one generation, because it is a question of growth, and every successive stage
of our political and economic development
gives it a new aspect, makes it a new question. The general lines of definition which
were to run between the powers granted to
Congress and the powers reserved to the
states the makers of the Constitution were
able to draw with their characteristic foresight and lucidity; but the subject-matter
of that definition is constantly changing,
for it is the life of the nation itself. . . . The
old measures of the Constitution are every
day to be filled with new grain as the varying crop of circumstances comes to maturity.

Woodrow Wilson
Constitutional Government in the United States
(1908)

THE NEW FEDERALISM

STATES' RIGHTS IN AMERICAN HISTORY

BY STEPHEN GOODE

A GROLIER COMPANY

FRANKLIN WATTS
New York / London / Toronto / Sydney
1983

For my mother,
Dorothy Vanscoy Goode

Library of Congress Cataloging in Publication Data

Goode, Stephen.
The new federalism.

Bibliography: p.
Includes index.
Summary: Describes the development of the relationship between the states and the federal government
throughout United States history and discusses the
present crisis in federalism in which President Reagan
seeks to reverse the centralization of power.
1. Federal government—United States—History—
Juvenile literature. 2. State rights—History—
Juvenile literature. [1. Federal government—History.
2. State rights—History] I. Title.
JK311.G66 1983 321.02′3′0973 82-21805
ISBN 0-531-04501-3

CONTENTS

THE NEW
FEDERALISM

CHAPTER ONE

REAGAN'S NEW FEDERALISM

...after fifty years of taking power away from the hands of the people in their states and local communities, we have started returning power and resources to them.

President Ronald Reagan
in his State of the Union Message
to Congress, January 26, 1982

In his 1982 State of the Union Message, President Reagan called upon Congress to support an ambitious new program designed to return power to state and local governments. "Our citizens," the President said, "feel they have lost control of even the most basic decisions made about the essential services of government, such as schools, welfare, roads and even garbage collection." Too much government planning was centered in the nation's capital by bureaucrats far removed from the concerns and needs of most Americans; too little was carried out in the state capitals or by city and county governments close to the people.

"A maze of interlocking jurisdictions," Reagan continued, ". . . confronts average citizens in trying to solve even the simplest of problems. They do not know where to turn for answers, who to hold accountable, who to praise, who to blame, who to vote for or against." The chief reason for this confusion, the President argued, was the vast increase in federal grants-in-aid programs, particularly over the past two decades. The national government had simply become too big and was no longer functioning as it should.

In 1960, Reagan pointed out, the federal government administered 132 grants-in-aid programs that cost $7 billion. By 1980— only twenty years later—these programs had more than tripled in number, to approximately 500, while their cost had grown by more than fourteen times the earlier amount, rising to nearly $100 billion. In the Congress, the President went on, "it takes at least 166 committees just to try to keep track of them." Since "neither the president nor the Congress can properly oversee this jungle . . . ," he concluded, "the growth of these grants has led to a distortion in the vital functions of government."

Reagan then quoted from the report of an intergovernmental commission set up to study the problems of government. The proliferation of federal programs in recent years, the report said, has made the federal government "more pervasive, more intrusive, more unmanageable, more ineffective, more costly and above all more unaccountable" than ever before.

But this excess of power, the President claimed, had not solved the nation's problems. On the contrary, the concentration of power in Washington had given America new problems to face, while leaving the old ones unanswered, and had undermined the traditional balance of power between the national government and the states.

How did President Reagan propose to alter this course of events? "Well, let's solve this problem with a single, bold stroke," he said, by returning almost half of the federal programs—some $47 billion worth—"to state and local government, together with the means to finance them and a transition period of nearly 10 years to avoid unnecessary disruption."

In his State of the Union message, the President did not have time to present the details of the complex plan he proposed, but promised that he would soon send Congress "a message describing this program." He emphasized, however, that his program would not be another solution to the country's woes drawn up in Washington and forced on the rest of the nation. His program, he said, could be "worked out only after close consultation with congressional, state and local officials." Only if there were input from all levels of government, could his program hope "to make government again accountable to the people" and "to make our system of federalism work again."

Reagan, however, did outline the main points of his new plan:

★ In October 1983—more than a year and a half away—the federal government would begin to take control of the entire Medicaid program, which provides health care to the poor. At the same time, the states would take over all the costs of the food-stamps program and of Aid to Families With Dependent Children, a major welfare program.

★ Also beginning in October 1983 the federal government would use the "full proceeds from certain excise taxes" to establish "a grass-roots trust fund that would "belong, in fair shares, to the 50 states." The total amount of money flowing into this fund, the President estimated, would be about $28 billion per year.

The states could use this trust fund in one of two ways. First, if the states wanted to continue to receive federal grants in areas like transportation, education, or social services, they could use the trust-fund money to pay for the grants. But second, if the states decided to forgo grants from the federal government, they could use the trust-fund money as they pleased, without interference from Washington.

By 1988, Reagan declared, "the states will be in complete control of over 40 federal grant programs." At that time, the trust would begin to be phased out, eventually to disappear entirely, and the states would take over the responsibility for the excise taxes to finance the programs. "They can then," the President concluded, "preserve, lower or raise taxes on their own, and find and manage these programs as they see fit."

Reagan called his program "bold" and "innovative." "In a single stroke," he claimed, "we will be accomplishing a realignment that will end cumbersome administration and spiraling costs at the federal level while we ensure these programs will be more responsive to both the people they are meant to help and the people who pay for them." The President added that he believed that the states and local communities were up to the "new and creative partnership" with the federal government that his program demanded. "This administration," he assured his listeners,

> has faith in state and local governments and the constitutional balance envisioned by the founding fathers. We also believe in the integrity, decency and sound good sense of grass-root Americans.

President Reagan implied that his new federalism could be seen as a second phase of what the press had dubbed the "Reagan Revolution." Phase One of the Reagan Revolution had been the President's highly controversial economic program, most of which had been passed by Congress in 1981.* Federal taxes had been cut by 25 percent over a three-year period and many long-standing federal programs in areas such as social and medical services, education, and energy had been drastically cut. Steps had likewise been taken to eliminate waste and fraud in government and to curtail government regulation of business and industry.

Phase Two of the Reagan Revolution would be the new federalism. For fifty years, Reagan believed, power had flowed to Washington. Now it was time to halt that trend. The Reagan

*For a discussion of the first phase of the Reagan Revolution see Stephen Goode, *Reaganomics: Reagan's Economic Program* (New York: Franklin Watts, Inc., 1982).

Revolution would be an unrelenting attack on big government and its aim, the President said, was to reinvigorate free enterprise, reawaken the self-initiative of the American people, and "bring America through this difficult time."

In the days following the President's message to Congress, Washington observers both attacked and praised the new federalism program. In the January 28, 1982, *Washington Post*, columnist Joseph Kraft wrote that the new federalism "may serve as a smoke screen obscuring the sinking economy and the hemorrhaging budget." By speaking of his new program at a time when the economy was in deep trouble and the federal deficit was growing at an alarming rate, Kraft charged, the President had dodged the most serious issues facing the country. The nation, he concluded, needed economic help, not a vast new plan to restructure federal and state relations.

But Bruce Babbitt, the Democratic Governor of Arizona, had kind words for Reagan's proposals. Writing in the same issue of the *Washington Post* in which Kraft's article appeared, Babbitt declared that the President's program "deserves a chance." Reagan, he continued, had "accurately characterized the problem" facing contemporary American government:

> *Since the New Deal, an accretion of more than 500 categorical programs has intruded the federal government into our lives at every level from the very important to the trivial. Congress does a little of everything, but hardly anything well. It ought to be worrying about arms control and defense instead of the potholes in the street. We might have both an increased chance of survival and better streets.*

"The president's proposal to restructure American government," Babbitt added, "is both elegant and imaginative" and "revolutionary in the best American sense of the word." It demanded that "Congress, the governors and state and local officials . . . rise to the occasion" and face the issue of federalism together. "At the very least," he concluded, Reagan "is entitled to a serious and thoughtful response from Congress and all elected officials."

What Is Federalism?

President Reagan has made his new federalism program a central part of his recipe for national revival. But what is federalism? Writing in *The Encyclopedia Americana*, the political scholar

William Livingston defines it as "the principle according to which two levels of government, general and regional, exist side by side in the state, each possessing certain assigned powers and functions."

Each of the two levels of government, Professor Livingston continues, "is limited to its own sphere and within that sphere is autonomous and independent; neither may arrogate to itself powers assigned to the other; each operates directly upon the people; and neither is dependent upon the other for its legislation, taxes, or administration."

In the American system of federalism, the two levels of government are the national and the state. The Founding Fathers outlined the role each level was to play in the Constitution. To the national government, they supplied what they hoped was sufficient power to create order and unity in the new nation and to provide security. To the states, they granted the right to maintain an independent political existence and to serve as centers of local government.

The dual system of government established by the Constitution was unique. Most of the governments of the time were highly centralized under a hereditary monarch or some other form of leadership. And where federal unions had existed—among the ancient Greek city-states and in the Holy Roman Empire—the balance of power between nation and state was vastly different from that created by the Founding Fathers.

What are the advantages of federalism and why did the Founding Fathers make it a central part of the Constitution? James Bryce, a nineteenth-century student of politics and an expert on the United States, discussed the attractions of federalism in his book *The American Commonwealth* (1888), widely regarded as one of the best works on America by a foreigner.

For the Founding Fathers, Bryce maintained, federalism furnished the means of uniting the thirteen original states "into one nation under one national government without extinguishing their separate administrations, legislatures, and local patriotisms." He believed that few Americans in 1789 would have approved of a strong central government, but found federalism acceptable because it preserved the autonomy of each of the states.

As a result of the federal system, Bryce went on, "every American citizen lives in a duality of which Europeans" have little or no experience. The American "lives under two governments and

[7]

two sets of laws; he is animated by two patriotisms and owes two allegiances."

> *That these should both be strong and rarely be in conflict is most fortunate. It is the result . . . above all of that harmony of each set of institutions with the other set, a harmony due to the identity of the principles whereon both are founded, which makes each appear necessary to the stability of the other, the States to the nation as its basis, the National Government to the States as their protectors.*

Bryce wrote that the Founding Fathers believed that federalism supplied the "best means of developing a . . . vast country" like the United States, because it allowed each state to meet its own problems in its own ways. Centralized governments, he noted, can be expected to be rigid and unimaginative, while state and local governments would tend to be "more truly natural and spontaneous" in dealing with new issues and crises.

Federalism made it possible for the states to experiment with a greater "variety of methods" and with "more adaptation of laws and administration" to varying circumstances than would be possible if there were but one central government with one overall policy for the nation. "Thus the special needs" of each state, he concluded, "are met by the inhabitants in the way they find best: its special evils are cured by special remedies . . . while at the same time the spirit of self-reliance among those who build up these new communities is stimulated and respected."

By allowing each state to pursue its own policies, Bryce added, American federalism created a laboratory where new social and political ideas could be tested. "A comparatively small commonwealth like an American State," he wrote, "easily makes and unmakes its laws; mistakes are not serious, for they are soon corrected. . . ." But most important, "other States profit by the experience of a law or a method which has worked well or ill in the State that has tried it."

If a policy has worked in one state, it can be adopted by others. If it has proved unsuccessful or disastrous, it can be avoided. Even the national government could profit by the example of the states by adopting what was good and rejecting what was bad.

Bryce believed that the characteristic that most strongly recommended federalism to the Founding Fathers was its tendency to prevent "the rise of a despotic central government." During

[8]

the Revolutionary War, he pointed out, Americans had fought to free themselves from what they regarded as the tyranny of the British Crown. In their Constitution, they adopted the federal principal which established the states as "bulwarks" against any expansion of power by the central government.

The state governments, Bryce said, were to act as a check and balance on the central government, preventing it from absorbing powers that belonged to the states and localities and from "menacing the private liberties of the citizen." The Founding Fathers, he concluded, regarded the power and independence of the states as essential to the American system because they believed that it was the states, and not the central government, that could best guarantee individual freedom and civil and property rights.

Finally, Bryce wrote, federalism was established in the United States because the Founding Fathers found that it was the best way to stimulate and maintain local self-government. "Self-government" was desirable, he claimed, because it encouraged "the interest of the people in the affairs of their neighbourhood, sustains local political life, educates the citizen in his daily round of civic duty," and "teaches him that perpetual vigilance and the sacrifice of his own time and labour" are essential to the practice of republican government.

Because federalism provided an environment in which the best kind of citizenship and public responsibility was fostered at all levels of government, it created citizens able to solve their own problems. And with so much political experience in existence at the local level, Bryce added, the national legislature was relieved "of a part of that large mass of functions which might otherwise prove too heavy for it. Thus business is more promptly despatched, and the great central council of the nation has time to deliberate on those questions which most nearly touch the whole country."

Federalism in American History
The Constitution of the United States only outlined the federal system. It defined the relationship between the nation and the states in general and sometimes vague terms that allowed for future change, reinterpretation, and evolution.

As a result, the practice of federalism in America has undergone constant alteration and revision. Some historical periods— usually those of national crisis like the Civil War and the Great

Depression—have stressed the importance of a strong centralized government with enough power to guide the nation through its problems. At other times, the significance of the states has been emphasized as a means to counter centralized power and renew individual liberty.

In the quotation cited at the beginning of this book, Woodrow Wilson noted the creative role federalism has played in American history. "The question of the relation of the states to the federal government," he wrote, "is the cardinal question of our constitutional system." But it was a question, he went on, that could not be "settled by the opinion of any one generation," because it was a "question of growth, and every successive stage in our political and economic development gives it a new aspect, makes it a new question."

Wilson believed that the framers of the Constitution "with their characteristic foresight and lucidity" provided "the general lines of definition which were to run between the powers" given to the nation and those exercised by the states. "But the subject-matter of that definition," he concluded, "is constantly changing, for it is the life of the nation itself. . . . The old measures of the Constitution are every day to be filled with new grain as the varying crop of circumstances comes to maturity."

In the early years of the Republic, the debate between national power and states' rights was carried on by the Hamiltonians, as the supporters of Alexander Hamilton were known, and the Jeffersonians, or followers of Thomas Jefferson. The Hamiltonians wanted a strong central government that would protect property, encourage business and commerce, and promote prosperity. Mistrustful of all authority, the Jeffersonians looked to the states to serve as barriers to national power and protect individual liberty.

Hamilton advocated a federalism in which the nation was supreme and spoke of the need for "vigor" and "energy" in the national government. It should never be forgotten, he wrote, "that the vigor of government is essential to the security of liberty" and that a good government must have "the power to serve the national interests." Furthermore:

A government ought to contain in itself every power requisite to the full accomplishment of the objects committed to its care, and to the complete execution of the trusts for which it is responsible, free from every other control but a regard to the public good and to the sense of the people.

[10]

Hamilton castigated those who feared "energy and efficiency in government" or who believed that centralized government automatically led to tyranny. An "enlightened zeal" for energy and efficiency in government, he said, was necessary if government was to work well. In his view, men were better off when they were less suspicious of government and more concerned with its good management.

Jefferson's views on federalism, on the other hand, were profoundly centered on the state and locality. His knowledge of world history led him to fear strong central government as a source of tyranny and despotism. Great political movements in the past, he pointed out, started with high ideals but ended up "with the governments preying on the people and the rich on the poor." His chief concern was to prevent such an occurrence from taking place in America.

In his essay entitled "Autobiography," Jefferson wrote that it was not by the "consolidation, or the concentration of powers . . . that good government" was established. Good government, he claimed, was created by the "distribution" of power throughout the nation and among as many centers as possible. In this way, he believed, individual freedom and liberty were best guaranteed and the chances that one man or group of men would seize control of the nation were lessened.

Jefferson's fear of the misuse of governmental power ran deep. To prevent the growth of tyranny, he advised that a "little rebellion now and then" was necessary. "The tree of liberty," he said, "must be refreshed from time to time with the blood of patriots and tyrants."

Throughout American history, Hamilton's vision of a strong central government has competed with Jeffersonian states' rights for the hearts and minds of Americans. The two men defined aspects of the American character that have always been in fitful and uncertain balance. When Americans assert the unlimited power of their country and its potential for commercial growth and prosperity, the Hamiltonian side is dominant. But when complaints of "get government off my back" and "that government governs best which governs least" are heard, the spirit of Jefferson has come to the fore.

The Present Crisis in Federalism
In the twentieth century three factors have worked to concentrate power in the national government. First has been the establish-

[11]

ment of the United States as a world power with far-flung interests and responsibilities. Second is the international crisis that began with the Great Depression and continued through World War II and the Cold War. And third is the enormous change that has taken place in communications and transportation since the time the Constitution was written in 1787.

America's emergence as a great power began in the 1890s and became a reality during World War I. In earlier years the United States had followed a policy of relative isolation from world affairs and was concerned primarily with its own affairs. Now American commercial enterprise and investment began to spread around the globe and the American government sought to exert its prestige and influence abroad. The power of the central government grew to meet this challenge.

But the greatest expansion of power in Washington came in the 1930s and afterward. In order to meet the problems of mass unemployment and economic stagnation created by the Great Depression, President Franklin Roosevelt, supported by Congress, established a host of federal programs designed to alleviate misery and stimulate the economy. No state government had proved equal to the crisis that faced the American people and in the absence of local action the national government moved in to take control.

The Great Depression was followed by World War II and the prolonged conflict between the Soviet Union and the United States known as the Cold War. In both cases, Washington was called upon to do what no state government was capable of doing. First, in World War II the resources of the nation had to be mustered against the combined threat of Nazi Germany, fascist Italy, and imperial Japan. Next, after the war American power was maintained to counter the expansion of communism throughout the world.

And as power concentrated in Washington to meet these great problems, revolutions in communications and transportation handed the national government even greater powers over American citizens. In 1787 it had taken many of the delegates several weeks to travel to Philadelphia to draw up the Constitution. The primitive transportation system and the lack of telegraph or telephone diminished the amount of power the central government could exert over the American people. In a very real sense, state government was more significant to most citizens than the national government because it was closer to them and could satisfy their needs more quickly and efficiently.

Modern communication and transportation devices, however, have erased old barriers of distance and time. The national government now has the ability to be nearer Americans than any state governments of the past. Within a short time, Washington can supply aid to the victims of earthquake or flood. Or it can initiate investigations into the lives of citizens suspected of wrongdoing. For better or worse, science and technology have rendered the national government extremely powerful.

Amidst this vast expansion of power in the central government, what has happened to the states? Since the 1930s the state governments have expanded their activities and made use of modern communication and transportation discoveries—but not to the same extent as Washington. The result has been a gap between national and state power: a crisis in the system of federalism envisioned by the Founding Fathers.

Many Americans have addressed themselves to this crisis. One of the most eloquent was John Harlan, who served as an associate justice of the Supreme Court between 1955 and 1971. In a series of dissents to majority opinions, Harlan voiced concern that the national government was destroying the "fabric of our federalism" and altering the relationship between the states and the nation. A true Jeffersonian, he feared that the destruction of federalism would mean the destruction of American liberty.

In 1962 Nelson Rockefeller, then governor of New York, took up the theme of federalism in his Godkin Lectures at Harvard University. Rockefeller offered a program he called "creative federalism" and which he believed would help revitalize the federalist system and give it new meaning in modern America.

Creative federalism, he said, would make use of all the levels and centers of power established by the Constitution. It would also make use of private centers of power like corporations and universities. Together, Rockefeller argued, these numerous centers of power would work as a "team" to solve the problems that faced the nation. In this "team" the national government would not always serve as the senior partner, but would bow to other centers of power when expertise lay elsewhere.

After 1964 President Johnson made Rockefeller's creative federalism a part of his social and economic program for the nation, and following Johnson, Presidents Nixon, Ford, and Carter took up the cause of federalism in one form or another. None, however, was able to halt the advance of the central government or bring it under control, or to restore a balance between national and state power that would satisfy the supporters of states' rights.

President Reagan's "new federalism" is the most ambitious program ever put forth to restore that balance of power. More deeply conservative than any recent president, he is committed to a limited and restrained exercise of power by the national government coupled with the restoration of the states to what he believes to be their proper place in the American system.

There is also another problem of federalism that the Reagan administration hopes to address. Over the past thirty years, the Supreme Court has been responsible for many changes in American life. Beginning with the landmark *Brown* decision of 1954 the Court has knocked down state laws regarding integration, criminal law, the apportionment of state legislatures and congressional districts, school prayer and Bible reading, the death penalty, and abortion.

During the same period the Court has likewise required the states to make new provisions regarding school busing, the makeup of state legislatures, and other problems once left to the states themselves to decide.

For many Americans these actions by the Court smack of what has been called "government by the judiciary." Federal judges, the critics point out, are not elected by the people, nor do they in any way represent public opinion. Federal courts should be in the business of interpreting the law, not making law and dictating social change.

The critics of the Court want its power limited. They support constitutional amendments to put an end to school busing and abortion and to permit prayer in public schools. Some urge Congress to pass laws restricting the authority of the Court to deal with certain issues they feel should be left up to the states.

President Reagan has proved sympathetic to many criticisms of the Supreme Court and has called for an amendment supporting school prayer. But his strongest influence over the Court will be in the appointment of new judges. He has already made one appointment—the moderately conservative Sandra Day O'Conner—and will likely have the opportunity to appoint others. His appointments will undoubtedly reflect his beliefs on federalism.

[14]

If Reagan achieves his "new federalism," he will indeed have accomplished a major turnabout in American history. This book will look at the changing attitudes toward federalism since the time of the Founding Fathers and conclude with a discussion of Reagan's new federalism and the questions it has raised in Washington and the states.

Can a more than fifty-year trend toward "big government" be reversed? Should it be reversed, if it means the possible destruction of numerous federal programs that support the needy and the sick? What possible role can the states play in a world in which the United States is a superpower and each state, taken individually, could be little more than a second-rate power or less?

And what position can the states play in a society in which scientific advances have made the national government an intimate part of the life of every American? What can be done — and should be done — about the exercise of power by the Supreme Court? The Reagan administration must address these and other similar problems as it attempts to create a new balance between the national government and the states. Clearly, the President's program is ambitious and will be difficult to carry out, but it is part of his vision of a revitalized America, a vision he has promised to accomplish.

I

UNITY OR DIVERSITY? THE DEVELOPMENT OF FEDERALISM

A nation, without a national government, is, in my view, an awful spectacle. The establishment of a Constitution, in time of profound peace, by the voluntary consent of the whole people, is a prodigy, to the completion of which I look forward with trembling anxiety.... because I know that powerful individuals, in this and in other States, are enemies to a general nation government in every possible shape.

Alexander Hamilton, *The Federalist*

Were not this country already divided into states, that division must be made, that each might do for itself what concerns itself directly, and what it can so much better do than a distant authority.... Were we directed from Washington when to sow, and when to reap, we should soon want bread. It is by this partition of cares, descending in gradation from general to particular, that the mass of human affairs may be best managed, for the good and prosperity of all.

Thomas Jefferson, "Autobiography"

CHAPTER TWO

THE QUEST FOR UNITY

It was ... thought that by the frequent meetings together of ... representatives from all the colonies, the circumstances of the whole would be better known, and the good of the whole better provided for; and that the colonies would, by this connexion, learn to consider themselves, not as so many independent states, but as members of the same body; and thence be more ready to afford assistance and support to each other, and to make diversions in favor even of the most distant, and to join cordially in any expedition for the benefit of all against the common enemy.

From the comments by Benjamin Franklin on the Albany Plan of Union of 1754

Before the Revolution, there was no American nation, no "united states." The English-speaking settlers who inhabited the eastern coast of North America regarded themselves as Virginians or Rhode Islanders, North Carolinians or citizens of Massachusetts. Each of the original thirteen colonies, from New Hampshire to Georgia, was a separate entity, largely self-reliant and proud of its own history, customs, and institutions.

Poor transportation and great distances caused the colonies to develop independently. England was an arduous sea voyage of six or more weeks away. For most of their early existence, the colonies were free of the heavy hand of Parliament or the Crown. By the 1760s and 1770s, when English demands on the American possessions began to increase, the tradition of isolation and self-reliance had become ingrained.

Poor transportation and great distances likewise separated the colonies from one another and allowed them to develop independently. The noted historian Page Smith has commented on the variety of traditions that characterized early American history. In their founding and development, Smith wrote in *A New Age Now Begins* (1976), there was a "remarkable diversity" among the thirteen colonies. "A number of human varieties and social forms, some as old as England itself, others as new as the new commercial and mercantile spirit of the age, were planted in the Virgin Soil of the New World."

In America, Smith continued, these human varieties and social forms "would grow luxuriantly, each in its particular way, in a vegetative mold made up of new ideas and opportunities." One colony would be shaped by "religious enthusiasm and rigid orthodoxy," while "tolerance and a vigorous commercial spirit would place an unmistakable stamp on another." The New World, he concluded, "was like some strange new garden where all kinds of transplanted vegetables and flowers lived together in vigorous incompatibility, growing with astonishing speed in that fertile ground and developing, in the process, new strains and varieties."

Virginia was founded by adventurers loyal to the Church of England, Massachusetts and much of New England by dissenters trying to escape that church. Maryland was a haven for Roman Catholics. Pennsylvania was the home of many Quakers. North and South Carolina were "proprietary colonies," begun by eight promoters who received the land from the Crown for payment of debts owed them. Georgia was in large part settled by debtors and others released from English prisons.

Differences in background and origin thus separated the colonies from one another, and the absence of any factors that might create unity and harmony allowed those feelings of separation to grow and become deeply rooted. Each colony had its own governor, its own judges, courts, and public officials. The colonies too had their own legislatures, where the colony's business and problems were discussed and debated.

By the time of the Revolution, the separation and individuality of the colonies had become part of the American way of life. Local self-government had become both a habit and an ideal— a tradition not easily shed to make way for a new and more centralized national government. The notion of states' rights, which has played such an important role in American history, had its origins in this early era when the colonies practiced a large degree of self-reliance and autonomy.

A First Attempt at Unity

Many factors caused the colonies to remain separate and distinct. There were other factors, however, which caused them to look to one another for mutual aid and assistance. One of these was the need for security against raids by Indians and other enemies. Another was common commercial and economic interests that could be resolved through mutual discussion and agreement.

In 1643, only twenty-three years after the settlement of Massachusetts, four colonies formed the New England Confederation. Massachusetts, Connecticut, Plymouth, and New Haven* banded

---

*Plymouth Colony was later absorbed into Massachusetts, and New Haven Colony became part of Connecticut.

together to form "a firm and perpetual league of friendship and amity, for offense and defense, mutual advice and succour."

The four colonies agreed to establish a central "commission" to which each colony would send two representatives. The purpose of the commission was to "hear, examine, weigh, and determine all affairs of war and peace." It was also allowed to "frame and establish agreements and orders in general cases of a civil nature" between the colonies in the Confederation and between the Confederation itself and other governments. Provisions were made for the admission of other colonies to the Confederation.

In order for the commission to approve a resolution, six of the eight commissioners had to agree. But once that vote of six out of eight was achieved, any resolution or plan of action passed by the commission was to be binding on all the members of the Confederation. Dissenting commissioners were expected to submit to the wishes of the six, and to bring the colonies they represented into line with the wishes of the commission.

During its forty-one years of existence, the New England Confederation was responsible for several notable accomplishments. It supported the establishment of Harvard College, the first institution of higher learning in the English-speaking colonies, and provided scholarships to that institution for worthy students. The Confederation likewise helped to settle boundary disputes, defended the settlers during the bloody Indian uprising of 1675–76, made laws concerning runaway servants, and established a fund for the conversion of Indians to Christianity.

But the Confederation also had its political problems and these problems involved states' rights. In 1653 one commissioner refused to be bound by the votes of seven other commissioners or to submit to their wishes. His failure to comply challenged the authority of the Confederation and made a shambles of the attempt to establish a meaningful and lasting unity among the member colonies.

The issue at hand was serious. The colonies of Connecticut and New Haven charged that the Dutch in New Amsterdam (now New York) had armed a number of Indians and enticed them to go to war against English-speaking colonists. Already several massacres of whites had occurred.

Seven of the eight members of the commission believed that

the Dutch "encroachments" called for a declaration of war on the part of the New England Confederation. The seven likewise supported plans for a military expedition against Dutch settlements. The eighth, however, a man from Massachusetts, disagreed. He refused to support the declaration of war. Moreover, he argued that the Confederation did not have the authority to require the allegiance of the colonies in matters as grave and serious as war.

The dissenting representative turned to the Massachusetts General Court for an opinion and the court supported him. The members of the Confederation, the Massachusetts court said, should not be bound by resolutions that are judged to be "manifestly unjust." The general court in each colony should have the right to determine what powers and authority the Confederation could exercise.

It was an "absurdity in policy," the decision continued, "that an entire government and jurisdiction" of an individual colony "should prostitute itself to the command of strangers" from other colonies. Furthermore, it was "a scandal to religion, that a general court of Christians should be obliged to act and engage upon the faith of six delegates against their conscience."

The decision concluded that in situations involving "the highest acts of authority" and "moral consideration"—such as the question of offensive war—the colonies had to remain supreme to the Confederation. "A fundamental law of a people or commonwealth," the court reasoned, "is, to have liberty and to exercise immediate choice of their own governors." Thus for Massachusetts to grant the New England Confederation any degree of authority over the people of Massachusetts was a "principle" that was "destructive" of the basic freedoms and liberties of the colony. The citizens of Massachusetts had to remain free to follow the dictates of their own conscience and beliefs.

The Confederation lasted for thirty years after the decision by the Massachusetts General Court, but much of the wind had been taken out of its sails. If the members of the Confederation could not rely on other members in time of need, then why belong to the Confederation? If a single colony could withdraw from a commitment it regarded as questionable, then the unity established by the Confederation would always be suspect and prone to disintegration.

The fate of the New England Confederation was the first example of a basic problem in American political history. Considerations of common defense and mutual economic interests dictated that the colonies unite and pool their resources. The fiercely independent colonies, however, regarded all talk of unity with distrust and abhorrence. Until some governmental system could balance unity with states' rights, few Americans would be interested in the establishment of a central authority.

The Albany Plan of Union

The New England Confederation dissolved in 1684, but the ideal of eventual union continued to exert its appeal. In 1697 William Penn, the founder of Pennsylvania and a popular colonial political leader, asked the British Board of Trade to establish a congress to which each colony, regardless of size, would send two delegates.

Penn saw the primary task of the congress as the arbitration and settlement of disputes between the colonies, since there was still no agency to carry out this responsibility. But he also wanted the congress to have the authority to "prevent or cure injuries in point of commerce," to provide defense against "public enemies," and oversee the extradition of criminals who had fled from one colony to another to escape justice.

The British Board of Trade, however, rejected Penn's proposal. It was easier—and less dangerous—for England to deal with the colonies individually; a united group of colonies might prove threatening and uncontrollable. In 1726 the call for union was taken up by Daniel Coxe, a son of one of the founders of the Carolinas. Author of a book titled *A Description of the English Province of Carolina,* Coxe argued for the creation of a "grand council" made up of two delegates from each colony.

The grand council was to be headed by a governor and would be concerned, above all, with defense. It would have the power to require each colony to supply quotas of men, money, and materiel to maintain an army. It would likewise have responsibility for the "jurisdictions, powers and authorities, respecting the honour of His Majesty, the interest of the plantations, and the liberty and property of the proprietors, traders, planters and inhabitants."

Coxe's plan for union had no immediate political influence on the colonies, but in 1754 his ideas and Penn's earlier proposals were taken up and expanded by Benjamin Franklin in what was known as the Albany Plan of Union. Franklin's proposals were

[25]

the most elaborate and significant plan for union yet put forth in the colonies, and it foreshadowed the federal government that was to be established after the United States won its independence from Great Britain.

The cause behind Franklin's call for union was fear of the French. The land west of the Alleghenies that lies between the Ohio Valley and the Great Lakes was claimed by Massachusetts, Virginia, and other English-speaking colonies. But the region was sparsely populated and its few English settlers were threatened by an alliance between the French and several Indian tribes, an alliance the French hoped would stall the expansion of the English colonies and cement their own claims to the area.

Alarmed by the French menace to English interests, the Board of Trade in London in 1753 ordered the royal governors of the thirteen colonies to meet with representatives of the Six Nations of the Iroquois at Albany in New York. The purpose of the meeting, according to London, was to "secure" the "wavering friendship" of the Iroquois before they too were brought under French influence.

Many colonial political leaders, however, came to the conclusion that the Indian question stood second to the problem of union among the colonies. This was the view of Governor William Shirley of Massachusetts, who spoke to his colony's assembly and asked its legislators to recognize the need for cooperation with the other colonies. "For forming this general union, gentlemen," Shirley said, "there is no time to be lost: the French seem to have advanced further toward making themselves masters of this Continent within the past five or six years than they have done ever since the first beginning of that settlement."

In June 1754 commissioners from nine of the thirteen colonies assembled in Albany for the congress. Only New Jersey, Rhode Island, Virginia, and Connecticut were absent. Four different plans of union were submitted for consideration by the commissioners, but Franklin's plan proved to be the most impressive. After agreeing upon several modifications, the congress adopted the Franklin proposals and called upon the colonies likewise to accept them.

The Albany Plan of Union asked for a "general government" that would encompass the thirteen colonies from New Hampshire to Georgia. At the head of the government there was to be a

"President-General" appointed by the king of England. There was also a "Grand Council," whose members were "to be chosen by the representatives of the people of the several colonies meeting in their respective assemblies."

Representation on the Grand Council was to be proportional and based on the contribution each colony made to the general treasury. No colony, however, was to have more than seven delegates or fewer than two. Massachusetts and Virginia, the wealthiest and most populous colonies, would have seven. New Hampshire and Rhode Island would have two.

Franklin believed that "frequent meetings" of the Grand Council would help the colonies to understand more clearly their common problems and circumstances and thus be better able to provide for "the good of the whole." What he wanted, he said, was for the colonies to "learn to consider themselves, not as so many independent states, but as members of the same body," ready to help and support one another.

The Albany Plan of Union endowed the general government with significant powers. The president-general, "with the advice of the Grand Council," possessed the authority "to hold or direct all Indian treaties in which the general interest of the colonies may be concerned; and make peace or declare war against Indian nations." The two divisions of government also had the power to regulate trade with the Indians, to purchase land from them for the British Crown and to make grants of that land to settlers.

But most significantly, the Albany Plan gave the general government the power to tax and to maintain an army. A general treasury was to be established and provided for by requisitions from the treasuries of the colonies. Furthermore, the general government could collect additional funds by levying such "general duties, imposts, or taxes" as appeared to it "most equal and just." Out of these funds, the government was to "raise and pay soldiers," provide for the erection of forts, and the maintenance of a coast guard.

To appease the colonies, the Albany Plan guaranteed that each colony would keep "its present constitution" and that existing military and civil establishments in the colonies would remain untouched. Furthermore, it provided that no citizen of any colony was to be impressed for military duty in the army of the general government without the consent of that colony's legislature.

But these were the only concessions to "states' rights." Franklin warned the Albany congress that if his plan for union were to work, it would have to be a strong one, binding on all its members. Recalling the fate of the New England Confederation, he pointed out that if one colony "on the least dissatisfaction" could withdraw from the union, then the union would "not be a stable one, or such as could be depended on" in time of crisis.

The commissioners left the Albany congress only to return home and discover their fellow colonists uninterested in the plan of union that had been decided upon. Not one colonial legislature ratified the program—in spite of the threat from the French and the Indians. The French and Indian War (1754–63) was waged by the colonies individually rather than in concert.

Historians believe that the Albany Plan failed for two reasons. First, the war scare did not affect each of the colonies in a similar manner. Franklin recognized this factor when he wrote several years later that "the colonies were seldom all in equal danger at the same time, or equally near the danger." Interest in union existed in direct proportion to the threat of war, and when that threat declined, the drive for union declined also.

But more important, the Albany Plan failed because it asked the colonies to give up too much of their authority to the general government. No colony that claimed land in the western territory wanted to see that land taken over and administered by the general government. Those claims, it was believed, belonged to the colonies individually, and not to the colonies as a whole.

Moreover, no colony wanted money from its own treasury turned over to a central treasury and none wanted to allow its citizens to be taxed by any government other than the local colony itself. The right to tax was a privilege jealously guarded by the colonies and they were reluctant to give up that privilege, even to a central government in which each colony was represented.

The Albany Plan's lack of success revealed how deeply the colonies were attached to their separateness and autonomy. Each colony viewed the others with suspicion and mistrust, and feared that it would have more to lose from a plan of union than it would gain. Not even the threat of imminent war was sufficient to bring them together.

During the first one hundred and fifty years of American history, the quest for unity failed to bear fruit. The New England

Confederation, the proposals of William Penn and Daniel Coxe, and the Albany Plan of Union each fell victim to the dominant trend of states' rights and local self-government. How that dominant trend was reversed and a balance struck between states' rights and the need for central government is the subject of the next two chapters.

CHAPTER THREE

INDEPENDENCE AND CONFEDERATION

You and I, my dear friend, have been sent into life at a time when the greatest lawmakers of antiquity would have wished to live. How few of the human race have ever enjoyed an opportunity of making an election of government, more than of air, soil or climate, for themselves or their children! When, before the present epocha, had three millions of people full power and a fair opportunity to form and establish the wisest and happiest government that human wisdom can contrive?

John Adams
Thoughts on Government
(1776)

The Declaration of Independence, adopted by the Continental Congress on July 4, 1776, spoke of "one People" who had found it "necessary . . . to dissolve the Political Bands which have connected them with another." It also referred to "these United Colonies." But there was still little real unity and Americans more often saw themselves as New Yorkers, Pennsylvanians, or Georgians than as "one people."

Indeed the Declaration stressed the separateness and individuality of the colonies by mention of the various "Forms of our Governments," the differing "Charters" and "valuable laws," and the thirteen distinct "Representatives Houses." The Declaration closed with a ringing call for independent states.

"We, therefore, the Representatives of the UNITED STATES OF AMERICA, in General Congress, Assembled," it declared, "appealing to the Supreme Judge of the World for the Rectitude of our Intentions, do, in the Name, and by Authority of the good people of these Colonies, solemnly Publish and Declare, that these United Colonies are, and of Right ought to be, Free and Independent States."

And as free and independent states, the document continued, "they have full Power to levy War, conclude Peace, contract Alliances, establish Commerce, and to do all other Acts and Things which Independent States may of right do."

Independence from Great Britain created three new problems for Americans to resolve. First, most states began to draw up new constitutions to replace the earlier colonial constitutions. Second, Americans had to decide what kind of central government, if any, they would have, and finally, they would have to face the difficult task of defining the relationship that would exist between that central government and the states.

The newly independent American people turned to the first problem with astonishing speed and devotion. In a short amount of time, most states adopted new constitutions that showed unusual political ability and wisdom. Into these constitutions Americans poured their belief in representative government, their hopes for liberty, and their willingness to experiment with new forms of political organization.

The problem of forming a central government, however, proved more elusive. Americans first adopted a form of federalism, known as the Articles of Confederation, in which the states were supreme. But when that system proved chaotic, unstable, and weak, they turned to another form of federalism under the Constitution in which the nation was supreme. With the Constitution, the American people hoped that a lasting balance had been struck between the need for a national government and the requirements of the states.

The State Constitutions

On May 10, 1776, the Continental Congress, a body of delegates from all thirteen colonies meeting in Philadelphia, recommended that each colony begin to consider a new form of government "as shall, in the opinion of the representatives of the people conduce to the happiness and safety of their constituents."

The recommendation was largely unnecessary. Already two colonies, New Hampshire and South Carolina, had drawn up new governments, and before the year was out, six more would follow their example. In 1780 Massachusetts became the last state to adopt a new constitution. In Europe and elsewhere the formation of the new governments was followed with interest. As James Madison noted:

> *Nothing has excited more admiration in the world than the manner in which free governments have been established in America; for it was the first instance, from the creation of the world . . . that free inhabitants have been seen deliberating on a form of government, and selecting such of their citizens as possessed their confidence, to determine upon and give effect to it.*

The new constitutions varied from completely new documents to slight modifications of the pre-existing colonial charters. But three stand out because of the influence they exerted and because of the political creativity they displayed. First, in order of time, was Virginia's, in which the state legislature was made powerful and the governor weak. Next was a radical constitutional exper-

[34]

iment in Pennsylvania, where the right to vote was extended to a wider segment of the male population than in any other state. And third was Massachusetts, the first American constitution in which the notion of "checks and balances" in government was brought elaborately into play.

★ *Virginia.* The framers of the Virginia Constitution, who included Patrick Henry and George Mason, made the state legislature supreme because they believed that the legislature, more than any other branch of government, reflected the will of the people. They divided the legislature into two houses, but gave the lower house the right to originate all legislation and have final say over the state budget because its members were elected from every county and were therefore closer to the people. The smaller upper house, with members elected from twenty-four districts, could consider legislation passed by the lower house, but could alter no bill pertaining to money and expenditures.

Virginia severely limited the power of its governor, and made him subject to the will of the legislature. He was to be elected every year by both houses, and he could serve no more than two successive terms, after which he had to be out of office four years before he could be re-elected. Moreover, he could do little without the advice and consent of the governor's council, a group of officials chosen by the legislature from among its own members and from "the people at large."

The most extraordinary part of the Virginia Constitution was its bill of rights. "All men are by nature equally free and independent," it began, and then went on to declare "that all power is vested in, and consequently derived from, the people." A list of freedoms and rights guaranteed to all citizens of Virginia followed.

The Virginia bill of rights guaranteed the right to a fair and "speedy" trial in capital and criminal offenses. It stated that a defendant could not "be compelled to give evidence against himself" and that "no man" could "be deprived of his liberty, except by the law of the land or the judgment of his peers."

It guaranteed freedom of the press and prohibited "cruel and unusual punishments." In spite of the Revolutionary War, which had already begun, it warned against "standing armies" as "dangerous to liberty" and stated that military authority should always be subordinate to civil authority. And, finally, the Virginia bill

[35]

of rights guaranteed that "all men are equally entitled to the free exercise of religion."

★ *Pennsylvania*. The constitution adopted by Pennsylvania reflected the victory of farmers, laborers, and other members of the lower classes over the commercial and social aristocracy that had earlier governed the state. It opened with a statement of thanks to God for "permitting the people of this State, by common consent, and without violence, deliberately to form for themselves such just rules as they shall think best for governing their future society."

The purpose of government in Pennsylvania, the document said, was "to establish such original principles...as will best promote the general happiness of the people of this State and their prosperity, and provide for future improvements, without partiality for or prejudice against any particular class, sect, or denomination of men whatever."

The framers of the Pennsylvania Constitution established a one-house legislature, believing that one house was more truly democratic than two. To eliminate secrecy in government, they required that the doors of the legislature had to remain open to all persons who behaved "decently" and that the "votes and proceedings of the General Assembly shall be printed weekly during their sitting, with the yeas and nays, on any question."

Furthermore, "all bills of a public nature" had to be "printed for the consideration of the people" before they were voted upon by the legislature and no bill could be passed into law until a sufficient amount of time had lapsed so that the people of the state could make their opinions on the issues known.

Executive power was placed in an elected council which each year selected one of its members to serve as president. In order to eliminate "the danger of establishing an inconvenient aristocracy," members of the executive council and of the legislature were rotated. Council members could serve only three out of every seven years; legislators could hold office only four years out of every seven.

Virginia and other states placed a property requirement on its voters. In Pennsylvania, every tax-paying male over twenty-one could vote, as could his adult sons. Finally, the Pennsylvania Constitution required the election every seven years of a "Council of Censors" which would "enquire whether the Constitution has been preserved inviolate in every part" and protect the people from the loss of their liberties and rights.

★ *Massachusetts.* Massachusetts went about the adoption of its constitution in a more systematic and democratic method than any other state. First, a constitutional convention was elected by manhood suffrage. The convention then appointed a committee to write the constitution. Finally, the document was debated, often clause by clause, in town meetings and accepted by statewide referendum.

The person largely responsible for the Massachusetts Constitution was John Adams, later the second president of the United States. Adams's views on politics were expressed in his *Thoughts on Government*, which he wrote to offer advice to the framers of the state constitutions. "There is no good government," he claimed, "but what is republican...because the very definition of a republic is 'an empire of laws, not of men.'" For Adams, "a republic of laws best secured for men the protection of their rights to life, liberty, and property."

Adams believed in the theory of "mixed government." According to this theory, each "pure" form of government—monarchy, aristocracy, and democracy—should be represented in the ideal government. Moreover, the three pure forms should be so "mixed" together that each had "checks and balances" on the others. Thus the monarchical element would be prevented from degenerating into tyranny, which it always had in the past; aristocracy would be prevented from becoming selfish oligarchic rule; and the tendency of democracy to become mob rule by the majority would be halted.

In the constitution Adams drew up for Massachusetts, "monarchy" was represented by the governor, who had far more power than any other state governor of the time and could veto legislation passed by the state legislature and appoint state officials. "Aristocracy" was represented by the upper house of the legislature, where men of property and education would sit. And "democracy" was represented in the popularly elected lower house.

Each of the three elements had powers that it could use against the others to prevent violations of a constitutional balance of power. No one element could grow excessively at the expense

[37]

of the others. To add further checks and balances, Adams established an independent judiciary that could act on its own, free of obligation to the chief executive or the legislature.

The Virginia Constitution, adopted in Richmond on June 29, 1776, influenced the writing of other state constitutions*, and its bill of rights, in varying forms, was adopted by each state, by the national government as the first eight Amendments to the Constitution, and by the French during the French Revolution. Pennsylvania abandoned its radical constitution in 1790 for a more conservative one, but not before Vermont had copied some of its radical features. And the Massachusetts Constitution, the brainchild of John Adams, proved to be very influential on the delegates assembled in Philadelphia in the summer of 1787 who drew up the Constitution of the United States.

Thus the states functioned as laboratories—centers of political invention and experimentation—out of which came many ideas important in American political history. At the state level, Americans seemed to feel free to exercise their political wisdom and try new forms of government. As John Adams wrote to his wife, Abigail, "We live in an age of political experiments. Among many that will fail, some, I hope, will succeed."

The Debate over a Central Government
But if Americans seemed inclined to experiment with forms of government at the state level, at the national level they proved more cautious and circumspect. Two views prevailed among the delegates at the nationwide Congress in Philadelphia in 1776. First was a group who favored a strong central government, a group historians have called the "nationalists." Second were the "anti-nationalists," or the supporters of states' rights and state sovereignty.

Nationalists like James Wilson, a prominent lawyer and delegate from Pennsylvania, believed that the Congress was superior to the state governments. The Congress, he told his fellow delegates, had responsibility for all Americans. In Congress, he said,

---

* North Carolina adopted its Constitution in December 1776. Like Virginia, North Carolina made the legislature supreme and severely weakened the authority of the governor. Indeed, his authority was so restricted that when one delegate to the North Carolina constitutional convention was asked by a friend just what role the governor could play in state government, the reply was "Why he can collect his salary."

[38]

"we are not so many states, we are one large state. We lay aside our individuality when we come here."

The nationalists also pointed out that a strong central government was necessary to promote commerce and foster trade. "Is it not necessary," asked Joseph Galloway of Pennsylvania, that trade . . . should be regulated by some power or other?" But "who shall regulate it?" he continued. "Shall the Legislature of . . . Georgia regulate it? Pennsylvania or New York?"

"No," Galloway answered, the regulation of American trade by each separate colony or state was unthinkable and unworkable. The "legislative powers" of the states "extend no further than the limits" of the states. Obviously, he concluded, the power to regulate trade must be placed in the hands of an authority that was superior to all the states and to which each state would submit. Galloway called this authority a national, or an "American," legislature.

For the anti-nationalists, on the other hand, the notion of a central government superior to the states was heresy. For them, in the words of Roger Sherman, a delegate from Connecticut, Congress was composed of "representatives of states" who had come together to discuss common problems. None of the thirteen states was inferior to the Congress and none had submitted any of its sovereignty to the Congress.

The anti-nationalists likewise had no sympathy with the notion that the different states would be made into one under a central government. Edward Rutledge of South Carolina warned the assembled Congress that a central government would destroy "all provincial distinctions" and make "every thing of the most minute kind bend to what they call the good of the whole." A nationalist system, he concluded, would sacrifice American liberty and diversity to rule by the majority.

Thus for the nationalists, a strong central government was necessary to provide security and stability and promote prosperity, but for the anti-nationalists, it was a threat to liberty and freedom, an evil that had to be avoided. Two people—John Dickinson and Thomas Burke—emerged as prominent spokesmen for both sides of the debate. Dickinson offered a plan to establish a strong central government. But after prolonged debate, the Congress, strongly influenced by Thomas Burke, radically altered the Dickinson plan to create a government in which the states were supreme and the central authority weak.

John Dickinson for the Nationalists

Dickinson, who was from Philadelphia, had been born in Maryland and educated in England. In 1767 he published *Letters from a Farmer in Pennsylvania,* one of the first works by an American author to be widely read in Europe. Deeply conservative and a monarchist at heart, he had at first voted against independence from Great Britain, but had sided with America once he saw his position go down to defeat.

Dickinson was chairman of the "drafting committee" of the Congress, charged with drawing up a plan of government for the independent states. Dickinson's plan placed significant powers in a central authority and weakened the powers of the states.

The Dickinson plan stressed the unity of the thirteen states. The colonies, it declared, "unite themselves so as never to be divided by any act whatever." At the head of the new government would be a national Congress in which each colony, regardless of its population, would have one vote.

Dickinson granted Congress the power to regulate trade and commerce. He also gave it the "sole and exclusive" right to enter into treaties with foreign nations and to settle "all disputes and differences now subsisting, or that hereafter may arise between two or more colonies concerning boundaries, jurisdictions, or any other cause whatever." Any treaties or judgments handed down by the Congress were to be binding on all the states.

Dickinson wanted Congress to establish an executive department which he called a "Council of States." The Council of States would be made up of members appointed by each state and would include "such committees and civil officers as may be necessary for managing the general affairs of the United States." The Council would operate all year round, and when the Congress was not in session, it would have charge of military and naval operations, make contracts, remove money from the national treasury, prepare matters for consideration by Congress, and call Congress into emergency meeting if events warranted it.

In the Dickinson plan, "each colony" was to "retain and enjoy as much of its present laws, rights, and customs, as it may think fit" and could reserve "to itself the sole and exclusive regulation and government of its internal policy." But at the same time, Dickinson made it clear that the states would have authority only in those "matters that shall not interfere" with the powers granted to Congress.

[40]

When state law "interfered" with national law, he concluded, national law must take precedence. The Dickinson plan, for example, specifically denied the states the power to levy duties or imports that would conflict with or hinder duties and levies already passed by the national Congress.

Thomas Burke and States' Rights

The Dickinson plan of government was first discussed by the Congress in Philadelphia during the summer of 1776. Opposition was mild and for a while the plan seemed destined for success. But in February 1777 Thomas Burke arrived to take his seat among the North Carolina delegation. An ardent supporter of states' rights, Burke immediately sensed the dangers the Dickinson plan presented to the states'-rights cause and urged his fellow delegates to reject its ratification.

Burke was a native of Ireland and a graduate of the University of Dublin. In the early 1760s he immigrated to America where he first practiced medicine and then turned to law and politics. He served in the North Carolina legislature and helped draw up his state's new constitution in 1776. After his term in Congress—where he quickly became the most articulate defender of states' rights—Burke returned to North Carolina and was elected governor. He died in 1783 at the early age of thirty-six.

From the moment he joined Congress, Burke opposed every effort to concentrate power in a new central government. His first notable achievement came three weeks after he took his seat, when Congress passed a resolution giving the national government the power to search out suspected deserters from the Revolutionary Army and bring them to justice.

For Burke, this resolution was anathema. Such power, he argued, belonged only to the states because only the states themselves had the right to "act coercively against their citizens." Congress could discuss problems common to all Americans, but it had no power to enforce national laws within state boundaries. To grant Congress this power, he concluded, would be tantamount to the destruction of "all the laws and constitutions of the states."

Burke called for a reconsideration of the question and the resolution was defeated. The states retained responsibility for army deserters. Burke told his fellow delegates that they had passed the resolution only because they had been "inattentive" to the dangers of centralized authority. "Civil authority," he said, "must be derived from the state" and never from the national government. Moreover, he added, the states must have the absolute right to set the "rules and limits" of their own internal affairs and Congress must never have power to alter those affairs.*

On March 11, 1777, almost two weeks after the desertion bill was defeated, Burke wrote a letter to the governor of North Carolina. In the letter he discussed his fears about Congress and centralized power in general. Most of the delegates he met in Philadelphia, he wrote, were full of "zeal for the public" and had "intentions" that were "generous" and "disinterested."

But the zealousness and devotion to duty of the delegates bothered him, Burke went on, because Congress dealt with political power and with the great issues of freedom and liberty. "Power of all kinds," he warned, "has an irresistable propensity to increase a desire for itself. It gives the passion of ambition a velocity which increases in its progress, and this is a passion which grows in proportion as it is gratified." In short, Burke argued, the more power Congress exercises, the more it will want.

Burke had no doubt that the more power Congress had, the more mischief it would do. "The more experience I acquire," he said, "the stronger is my conviction that unlimited power can not be safely trusted to any man or set of men on earth." The reason men could not be trusted with power, he wrote, was that power gave them a "delusive intoxication" which distorted their beliefs and caused them to turn their backs on what they once held true.

"I believe," he concluded,

...the root of the evil is deep in human nature. Its growth may be kept down but it cannot entirely be extirpated. Power will sometime or other be abused unless men are well watched, and checked by something they cannot remove when they please.

---

* Burke's attack on centralized government fell on sympathetic ears. Many delegates had already been instructed by their state legislatures to support states' rights. Virginia told its delegates that "the power of forming a government for, and the regulations of the internal concerns of each colony" should "be left to the respective colonial legislatures." Maryland, North Carolina, Rhode Island, and Pennsylvania gave their delegates similar instructions.

Burke maintained that the powers of Congress should be "accurately defined" and that there should be an "adequate check provided to prevent any excess."

"Men so eminent as members of Congress," Burke warned, bear close watching because they "are willing to explain away any power that stands in the way of their particular purposes." Unless Americans constantly remembered and practiced their custom of local self-government, he continued, the exercise of power by Congress would become "firm in habit, and men will be accustomed to obedience" to a national authority. The price of liberty was constant vigilance against the encroachments by the national government.

In a nutshell, Burke had stated the central argument of the states'-rights cause: Americans had not overthrown the tyranny of the British Crown to replace that tyranny with another instituted by Congress. The states must remain free and independent to act on their own and thus serve as a strong counterweight to centralized authority.

But there was also another states'-rights argument that carried weight with the delegates in Philadelphia. In the past, genuine representative government had flourished only in small states. It had been lost when those states became large and oppressive. Athenian democracy had been swallowed up by the empire of Alexander the Great. The Roman Republic disappeared when the Roman Empire was declared.

If history were any guide—and many early Americans believed that it was—then representative government had a far greater chance of survival at the local level than at the national. American freedom and liberty could best be guaranteed by state authority, which was close at hand and accountable, than by a centralized authority that was remote and distant.

The Articles of Confederation
In April 1777 Congress again took up discussion of the Dickinson plan. This plan, Burke told the delegates, offered American citizens a clear choice. Congress and the national government could be supreme, as the plan envisioned, or the delegates could drastically alter and amend the plan to protect states' rights and state sovereignty.

The delegates chose to amend the plan. By an overwhelming

majority,* they accepted a plan of government called the "Articles of Confederation and Perpetual Union." Thomas Burke drew up a statement, which was accepted by the Congress, that made the power of the states supreme. "All sovereign power," the statement said, "was in the states separately." Congress and the states could exercise a few "expressly enumerated" powers jointly, "but . . . in all things else each state would exercise all rights and power of sovereignty uncontrolled."

The Articles of Confederation called the new nation "The United States of America" and defined its government as a "league of friendship" established by the states "for their common defense, the security of their liberties, and their mutual and general welfare." The word "league" emphasized that the union would be a combination of separate and equal states, and not a single, unified nation.

As Burke had wanted, the Articles carefully enumerated—and limited—the powers granted to the national Congress. Congress was to have "the sole and exclusive right and power" of declaring war or making peace. It could send and receive ambassadors and enter into treaties and alliances. It could regulate the value of coinage issued by the Confederation and the separate states and was given the responsibility of establishing a uniform system of weights and measures for the whole country. It could likewise establish post offices.

But over each of these powers, the states were given significant control. In Congress, each state could have between two and seven delegates, depending on the size of the state. The method of electing delegates was to be determined by the states themselves and each state had the right to withdraw its delegates at any time, if those delegates failed to live up to their commitments.

Voting in Congress would be done by states, with each state, large or small, having one vote. In all "important matters," like war and peace and military affairs, the approval of nine of thirteen states was necessary for passage of a new bill. In lesser matters, such as the postal system, seven votes were required. An amendment to the Articles of Confederation required unanimous consent

---

* The vote was eleven states to one, because the delegates voted by states and not individually. New Hampshire's delegation divided evenly for and against and so New Hampshire's vote was not counted. Only among the Virginia delegation did a majority of delegates vote against the Articles of Confederation.

by the thirteen states, a fact that virtually assured that the Articles would not be altered, since complete agreement among the states on any issue was unlikely.

The Dickinson plan had envisioned a "Council of States" that would serve as an executive branch and help Congress run the nation. The Articles of Confederation instead established a "Committee of States" which sat only when Congress was not in session and could deal only with matters of minor importance. It could not, for instance, make decisions regarding war and peace, even in time of crisis.

The powers the Articles *denied* to Congress were significant. Congress could not tax, but had to rely on requisitions from the states to fill the national treasury. Moreover, Congress was given no authority to deal with paper money issued by the thirteen states and it could not interfere with state laws regarding exports and imports, imposts or duties, or establish a uniform regulation of trade for the whole country.

Congress was given the power to settle disputes between the states. But it could discuss these disputes only when the states involved petitioned for arbitration, and even then, the states were not required to follow any rulings that Congress might hand down.

Thus the government established by the Articles of Confederation was a two-leveled, federal system in which the states were supreme. Congress was permitted to do little more than *manage* national affairs. Legislative and lawmaking power resided primarily in the states. As historians have noted, the Articles gave Congress the right to discuss issues, but no power to compel the states to obey its opinions.

The Articles of Confederation represented a victory of the antinationalists over the nationalists and those who favored a strong centralized authority. The tradition of states' rights had won; a government had been established in which, in the words of John Witherspoon, the president of Princeton University and a delegate to Congress, every state was a "distinct person."

CHAPTER FOUR

TOWARD A MORE PERFECT UNION

The deliberate union of so great and various a people in such a place is, without all partiality or prejudice, if not the greatest exertion of human understanding, the greatest single effort of national deliberation that the world has ever seen.

John Adams
December 26, 1787

WE THE PEOPLE *of the United States, in order to form a more perfect union, establish Justice, insure domestic tranquility, provide for the common defence, promote the general Welfare, and secure the Blessings of Liberty to ourselves and our Posterity, do ordain and establish this Constitution for the United States of America.*

The Preamble
to the Constitution

Writing in the July 10, 1981, issue of one of America's leading conservative magazines, *The National Review,* historian Thomas Wendel noted that it was "particularly fitting that the Reagan Administration takes office in this two-hundredth anniversary year of the Articles of Confederation."* Under the Articles, Americans organized a new government, a government that emphasized states' rights. Similarly, Wendel went on, the Reagan administration wants to reorganize government, "reverse the trend toward centralization," and "in the spirit of the Articles" revive "the philosophy of . . . self-government" at the state and local level.

Wendel acknowledged that the Articles of Confederation were an experiment in government that had flaws and ultimately failed. But he nevertheless pointed to several important achievements made by the new nation in spite of those flaws. Under the Articles, America had waged a successful War of Independence against Great Britain, a major power of the time, and concluded an honorable peace.

Under the Articles, too, Congress had provided that new states would be admitted to the union on a basis of equality with the original thirteen states, prohibited slavery in any state formed from the territory north of the Ohio River, and made plans for the development of public education in the same area. These accomplishments, Wendel wrote, were important because they "guaranteed that the United States had a future."

But the most significant achievement of the Articles of Confederation, according to Wendel, was that they established "federalism"—"the doctrine of divided sovereignty"—as the American system of government. By affirming the importance of states'

---

*Congress agreed upon the Articles in 1777, but they were not officially adopted until 1781, when Maryland became the last state to ratify them.

rights and defining the two-leveled relationship between the states and the nation, the Articles set the course American political history would follow. Later events would modify that relationship and play down states' rights, but it was the Articles that supplied the original framework of federalism.

The Weaknesses of the
Articles of Confederation

Wendel's positive assessment of the Articles comes from a vantage of two centuries. For many prominent Americans of the 1780s, however, the Articles were an abomination and a curse. James Madison, a hard working member of Congress from Virginia, regarded them as full of "embarrassments and mortal diseases." Alexander Hamilton found them worse than no government at all.

George Washington feared that the new national government was too weak and disorganized to meet the challenges it would have to face. Benjamin Franklin publicly professed his scorn for the Articles. Franklin claimed that he could not understand why Americans took pride in first defining themselves as "Virginians" or "Rhode Islanders." There was a deeper political reality, he said, that made all Americans one people rather than citizens of separate states.

Critics found four fatal flaws in the Articles of Confederation that needed alteration. First was the inability of the national government under the Articles to provide security and develop a strong army and navy. Second was the new government's lack of fiscal responsibility. Third and fourth were its powerlessness in the supervision of trade and commerce and the establishment of a successful foreign policy.

Inadequacy During War. Congress appointed George Washington to command a unified army during the Revolutionary War, but throughout the war Washington complained that he felt more like the commander of thirteen separate armies than of one national army. His work, he believed, had been rendered unduly complex and difficult because he had to deal with each state individually in order to outfit and equip his army.

Congress required each state to supply a quota of men to the army, but these quotas were never filled and Congress had no power to enforce them. The army was to number 20,000—out of a population of 3,000,000—but never had more than 14,000 soldiers at one time. In 1781, the sixth year of the war, Washington noted in his diary that the army had shrunk to a dangerously low level of manpower and that no state had more than one-eighth of its quota of men in the field.

Moreover, no state fulfilled its quota of food, clothing, and other necessities used to supply and maintain the army. Washington frequently protested the shortages, but to no avail. The states were more likely to provision their own state militias than the national army.

In 1779 several members of Congress prepared a statement which declared that "the inattention of the states has almost endangered our very existence as a people." The statement, however, was never released for fear it would anger the supporters of states' rights and make waging the war more difficult.

At the end of the war, Washington wrote that if Congress and the national government had been better organized and more efficient in creating an army and unifying the people,

we should not have been for the greater part of the war inferior to the enemy, indebted to our safety to their inactivity, enduring frequently the mortification of seeing inviting opportunities to ruin them pass unimproved for want of a force which the country was completely able to afford, and of seeing the country ravaged, our towns burnt, the inhabitants plundered, abused, murdered, from the same cause.

Fiscal Irresponsibility. The government incurred a debt of $42 million during the Revolutionary War, mostly from Dutch and French sources. The Articles, however, granted Congress no power to tax the people of the United States. Only the states had that power. The national treasury was to be filled by requisitions from state treasuries.

But once again the states failed to live up to what was required of them. No state gave its total obligation to the national treasury, and some gave nothing at all. The Articles provided no means for Congress to force the state governments to turn over the money.

Congress attempted to amend the Articles so that it could raise money by levying a tax on foreign imports, but the amendment was vetoed by Rhode Island, which believed that only the states should have the right to tax imports. Nor did Congress have the means to service the national debt, because supporters of states' rights believed that this would put too much power in the hands of the central government.

In these circumstances, the credit of the new nation declined. Foreign creditors pressed for payment of debts. Even American soldiers who fought in the Revolutionary War could not be paid. In 1783 Congress was forced to move from Philadelphia to Princeton, New Jersey, because of threat of attack by soldiers demanding back salaries.* Three years later, in 1786, with the nation facing bankruptcy, a congressional committee declared the time "had arrived when the people of these United States, by whose will, and for whose benefit the federal government was instituted, must decide whether they will support their rank as a nation."

Problems with Trade and Commerce. The Articles of Confederation gave Congress no power to regulate trade and commerce or to control the issuance of paper money by the states. The result was economic disorder and uncertainty.

Each state developed its own set of commercial laws and regulations that often conflicted with those of other states. Each state too printed its own paper money which gave the nation thirteen different paper currencies that fluctuated widely in value and were often quite worthless. In banking and business transactions, Americans frequently had to rely on foreign money of known and respected international value.

In these circumstances, Congress could do little or nothing to encourage American commerce and trade or to promote prosperity. British trade continued to dominate the New World. After the Revolutionary War, which had ravaged parts of the nation,

---

*As if to underline the unimportance of the national government, the Articles of Confederation provided for no permanent home for Congress. After being forced from Philadelphia to Princeton, Congress then moved to Annapolis, Maryland. From Annapolis it moved to Trenton, New Jersey, and then to New York—five different locations in less than four years.

the United States experienced a prolonged economic depression which Congress was powerless to alleviate.

Foreign Affairs. One of the few powers the Articles granted exclusively to Congress was control of foreign affairs. Treaties accepted by Congress were to be binding on the states and no state was permitted to pass laws that violated agreements and stipulations made in those treaties. But even this clearly worded mandate was ignored by the states.

The 1783 Treaty of Paris, which ended the American Revolution, stipulated that both American and British creditors would receive full value for the debts owed them before the war broke out. Furthermore, the treaty stated that the property that belonged to Americans who remained loyal to Great Britain would not be confiscated and that the loyalists would be allowed to travel unhampered in the United States to claim their property.

Soon, however, it became obvious that the states were not going to live up to these promises, although Congress had voted to accept the treaty. Virginia forced its loyalists to leave the state with no compensation for property. New York passed stiff fines to punish its loyalists. Elsewhere the lives of loyalists were threatened by mobs. By 1786 John Jay, who had helped to negotiate the treaty, could declare that from the time of its ratification, not one day had passed when the treaty had "not been violated by one or other of the states."

With America failing to live up to its end of the bargain, Great Britain refused to live up to its. As part of the settlement, the British had promised to remove their troops from the United States. Now they announced that British troops would remain in the Northwest Territory—a part of the United States—in order to protect the lives and property of the loyalists. Furthermore, British ships would remain on the Great Lakes.

A sizable British military and naval presence so near the thirteen original states threatened American liberty. Would the English make use of their forces if further violations of the Treaty of Paris occurred? Congress was powerless to deal with the problem—unless some means were found to strengthen the national government so that it could provide adequate security and defense and so that it could force the states to abide by treaties the Congress had passed into law.

The Call for a New Plan of Union

Concern about the condition of American society under the Articles of Confederation came to a head in 1786, when rebellion broke out in western Massachusetts. Economic hard times had hit America and in New England many farmers lost their land because they had no money to pay their taxes.

Angered by the failure of the legislature to come to their aid and support them in time of need, bands of farmers of Massachusetts took up arms. Led by Captain Daniel Shays, the rebels hoped to close down the county courts and thereby prevent any further foreclosures and loss of property. If the state failed to protect their interests, the farmers declared, then they would take matters into their own hands.

In 1786 and 1787 the rebellion continued, sometimes involving as many as fifteen hundred farmers. Massachusetts seemed unable to handle the problem and Congress was too weak to supply needed help.

Said George Washington from his estate in Virginia, "It was only the other day that we were shedding our blood to obtain the constitutions under which we live—constitutions of our own choice and making—and we are now unsheathing the sword to overturn them."

In 1787 the rebellion was put down by a militia financed by forced contributions from Boston merchants—but not before it had influenced public opinion throughout the United States. The failure of Congress to come to the aid of Massachusetts underlined the weaknesses of the Articles of Confederation. If the Congress was unable to provide security in time of crisis, then the national government had to be strengthened.

Fortunately, there was already a movement in progress to bring the states together to discuss the nature of their relationship. In 1784 and 1785, at the instigation of James Madison and George Washington, representatives from Maryland and Virginia met to discuss common problems of the two states. The talks were so successful that the Virginia legislature called for a nationwide meeting of states "to consider how far a uniform system in their . . . commercial regulations may be necessary to their . . . permanent harmony."

In September 1786 representatives of five states met in Annapolis, the capital of Maryland. Four other states had named

representatives who failed to arrive and four named no representatives at all. But in spite of the small turnout, the work of the
Annapolis Convention was to prove important. Before disband-
ing, the delegates called for a meeting of all the states in Philadelphia in 1787. The purpose of this meeting, they declared,
would be to look into the flaws of the Articles of Confederation
and find ways to correct them.

The New Federalism of 1787

The November 6, 1786, edition of the *New-Jersey Gazette,* published in Trenton, carried a letter by an anonymous writer that
summed up the feelings of many Americans of that time. "The
American war" with Great Britain, the writer declared, is long
over, "but this is far from being the case with the American
Revolution. . . . It remains yet to establish and perfect our new
forms of government."

When the delegates assembled in Philadelphia in May of 1787,
it had been almost eleven years since the Declaration of Independence had severed America's ties with Great Britain. Ten
years had passed since Congress had adopted the Articles of
Confederation. But the formation of an adequate and efficient
government still eluded the American people.

Every delegate at the convention agreed that some new balance
had to be struck between the states and the national government.
But what was this balance to be? On this question, the delegates
had markedly differing opinions.

A few ardent nationalists were in favor of doing away with
the states almost entirely. George Read of Delaware, for instance,
complained to the convention that "too much attachment" had
been expressed for the state governments. "We must look beyond
their continuance," he said, and establish a strong centralized
government "on new principles." Otherwise, "we must either go
to ruin, or have the work to do over again."

James Madison, however, told the delegates that he found the
idea of the "consolidation" of the states into "one simple republic"
to be both "unattainable" and "inexpedient." Any plan of government the convention adopted, he argued, would have to include the states, because they were political entities of long standing
and should not be dissolved overnight to create an entirely new
nation.

But if the states were to be included in the new government, what role were they to play and what voice were they to have in national affairs? On these questions, too, the delegates were deeply divided.

Madison favored a system of federalism in which what he called the "national authority" was supreme but that did "not exclude the local authorities wherever they can be subordinately useful." His plan of union—known as the Virginia Plan—gave significant powers to the national legislature.* Madison wanted a Congress that could pass laws "in all cases to which the separate states are incompetent, or in which the harmony of the United States may be interrupted" by individual state laws.

But Madison included proposals in the Virginia Plan that proved highly controversial. First, he insisted that Congress have the power to "negative" all state laws that interfered with national law. This power, he believed, was necessary if Congress was to be able to enforce its will on the states.

Second, Madison wanted the members of both houses of Congress to be chosen on the basis of population. There was no reason, he said, for a large state like Virginia, with its 800,000 inhabitants, to have the same voice in Congress that Delaware had with its 60,000 or Georgia with its 80,000. In order to give every American an equal voice in the national government, representation had to be based on population.

The Virginia Plan quickly aroused the fears of delegates from small states. William Paterson of New Jersey denounced it as an effort by the large states to "swallow up" less populated states. If Virginia, Pennsylvania, and other large states had more votes in Congress than the small states, he pointed out, they would be able to outvote the small states on every issue and the small states would end up with no power at all. Paterson wanted all states, regardless of size, to have the same vote in Congress.

Gunning Bedford, a delegate from Delaware, was likewise deeply opposed to the Virginia Plan. If the large states insisted on having their way, he warned, the small states would have no choice but to leave the union and find some other means to protect their security and liberty. Perhaps, he added, they could "find

---

*Madison's plan of government reflected the Virginia Constitution, which he had helped to write. Both the Virginia Plan and the Virginia Constitution stressed the importance of the legislature, which they viewed as "the voice of the people."

some foreign ally of more honor and good faith, who will take them by the hand and do them justice."

The Great Compromise

A compromise between the demands of the large states and those of the small states was first suggested by John Dickinson, the author of the Dickinson plan of union of 1776. Dickinson proposed that membership in one house of Congress be based on population, while in the other house, each state would have an equal vote. This solution, he claimed, would satisfy both sides in the dispute, because it would make both proportional representation and equality of representation a part of the new government.

Dickinson's proposal impressed the delegation from Connecticut—a small state—and the Connecticut delegates began to urge its acceptance by the convention. But it took more than two weeks of difficult and sometimes rancorous debate before a compromise was reached. Many delegates from large states held out for proportional representation to the end, when they were defeated by a combination of small states.

The Great Compromise, as historians have called it, established a House of Representatives whose membership was elected on the basis of population, and a Senate in which each state had two votes. In the House, the states were allowed one representative for every thirty thousand citizens. Until a census could be taken, Virginia was granted ten, Rhode Island and Delaware one each, and the other states various numbers in between. In the Senate each state, regardless of size, was to have two senators.

Summing up the advantages of the Great Compromise, Oliver Ellsworth of Connecticut said that "the proportional representation in the first branch was conformable to the national principle and would secure the large states against the small." At the same time, he added, the "equality of voices" in the second branch "was conformable to the federal principle and was necessary to secure the small states against the large."

The Constitutional Convention likewise varied the role of the House and Senate in other ways. The House of Representatives was allowed to originate all bills concerning money, appropriations, and expenditures. The Senate, on the other hand, had the power, along with the president, to make treaties and approve of nominations to the Supreme Court.

[57]

Moreover, members of the House and Senate were to be elected in different ways, reflecting the differing roles the two bodies played. The Senate was regarded as a more "aristocratic" and select body than the House of Representatives. According to Gouverneur Morris of Pennsylvania, one of the most conservative delegates at the convention, the Senate's duty would be "to check the precipitation, changeableness, and excesses" he feared the House would be prone to commit.

Responsibility for the selection of senators was therefore turned over to the state legislatures. This was done for two reasons. First, the Senate was to be the repository of state power and interests and it was therefore wise to let the state legislatures have a say over who sat there. Second, it was believed that the legislatures would tend to choose only the ablest, best-educated, and most-experienced men to represent their states. Senators would have terms of six years.*

An entirely different principle was adopted for the selection of members of the House of Representatives—the principle of popular election. Representatives were to be chosen every two years and their elections were to be open to any citizen qualified to vote for the members of the "most numberous Branch of the State Legislature" of the state in which he resided.

A few conservative delegates at the convention had wanted the state legislatures to select House members, but not Elbridge Gerry of Massachusetts. Gerry numbered himself among the conservatives—Shays' Rebellion in his home state, he said, had caused him to fear democracy—but he feared state legislatures more than he feared popular vote.

"In Massachusetts," he said, "the worst men get into the Legislature. Several members of that body," he continued, have "lately been convicted of infamous crimes." They were men of "indigence, ignorance, and baseness," who spared "no pains, however dirty to carry their point against men who are superior." Gerry strongly supported the popular election of House members so that they would be as free as possible from control by corrupt state legislatures.

---

*In order to give as much stability and continuity to the Senate as possible, the Constitution arranged the terms of senators so that only one-third of the Senate is elected every two years, leaving two-thirds to carry on business without disruption. By contrast, all members of the House of Representatives must stand for election every two years.

James Madison suggested another reason for popular elections. "All civilized Societies," he said, are "divided into different Sects, Factions, and interests." There are "rich and poor, debtors and creditors, the landed, the manufacturing, the commercial interests, the inhabitants of this district or that district. . . ."

A republican form of government, he continued, must guarantee that each of these interests is represented. Moreover, it must see that no group of interests unites to form a majority that prevents minority interests from voicing their needs and views.

How were these tasks to be accomplished? The best way to protect the interests of everyone, Madison argued, was "to enlarge the sphere" of voters to encompass as much of the population of the nation as possible. In that way, all opinions would have a chance to be aired. But at the same time, the "community" would be divided "into so great a number of interests and parties" that it would be difficult to form a majority that could tyrannize or dominate a minority interest.

Madison believed that the House, because its membership was based on popular election, would function as the voice of the people. It was the one branch of the government elected by a sphere of voters large enough to encompass the variety of American society. Its responsibility to all the people, he concluded, would render it "both a safe and competent guardian of the interests which will be confided to it."

The Great Compromise was at the heart of the federalism established by the Constitution of 1787. It affirmed the existence of the states as traditional political units essential to the American system and gave them an equal voice in the Senate. But it also affirmed the existence of Americans as one people and one nation, united, with a single destiny—and gave that people a voice in the House of Representatives. The Great Compromise combined the thirteen states and the nation into what one delegate at the Convention called "one political society."

The Division of Power
The framers of the Constitution had succeeded in finding a means to represent both state and national interests in Congress. But they likewise had to face another difficult problem. In order to strengthen the central government and make it more effective, certain powers that the states had enjoyed under the Articles of Confederation had to be taken away and granted to the nation.

How was this to be done without arousing the anger and opposition of the supporters of states' rights?

The answer was: carefully and cautiously. The framers were careful to delegate to the nation only specifically enumerated powers which they listed in Article I, Section 8, of the Constitution. All those rights and powers not listed in that section were to remain with the states. At the same time, the framers of the Constitution were also careful to allow the states a voice in almost every exercise of authority that the national government might undertake, so that state and national power were intimately and inextricably woven together.

The Constitution granted Congress powers that had been missing under the Articles of Confederation. It had the power "to lay and collect Taxes, Duties, Imposts and Excises." It likewise had the power "to regulate Commerce with foreign Nations, and among the several States" and to establish an army and a navy. These powers, and others, were to be exercised jointly by the House, in which representation was on the basis of population, and by the Senate, in which each state had an equal voice.

The Constitution spelled out national powers as clearly as possible.* But it made no list of the powers granted to the states. It was simply assumed that the states would continue to exercise all those powers and functions they had exercised before the Constitution—except for the powers that had been given the national government. The states would maintain control of their own internal affairs, from the regulation of commerce within the state to education, state judicial systems, and other local matters.

Article I, Section 10 of the Constitution specifically denied certain powers to the states. No state, for instance, was permitted to "enter into any Treaty, Alliance, or Confederation" or to "coin Money." Nor could any state, "without the Consent of the Congress, lay any Imposts or Duties on Imports or Exports." These restrictions on state power helped to eliminate the financial and

*At least two of the powers granted Congress were so open-ended that they could (and have been) interpreted as permitting an almost unlimited expansion of congressional authority. First was the power "to regulate Commerce . . . among the several States. Second was the last power listed in Article I, Section 8, which gave Congress the right "to make all Laws which shall be necessary and proper for carrying into Execution the foregoing Powers, and all other Powers vested by this Constitution in the Government of the United States, or in any Department or Officer thereof." Supporters of a strong national government have used these powers to concentrate power in the central government.

commercial problems that had arisen under the Articles of Confederation.

The Constitution established two new branches of the national government that had not existed under the Articles of Confederation: the executive and the judiciary. But the states were given power to influence both through the way the president and federal judges were chosen and through the power Congress had over the other two branches.

The president, for example, was to be voted upon by "Electors" from each state who were appointed "in such Manner as the Legislature thereof may direct." Each state had electors equal to the total number of representatives and senators it had in Congress. Every four years, the electors would meet in their home states to cast their votes for the presidential candidate of their choice.

But the states also had other controls over the selection of the president. If two or more candidates tied in the number of electoral votes they received, the Constitution required that the election be decided by the House of Representatives. In such cases, each state delegation in the House was to have only one vote, assuring the small states a voice equal to that of the large states.

Moreover, the power exercised by a president, once he was elected, was far from absolute. He could veto legislation passed by Congress, but Congress could override that veto by a two-thirds vote of both Houses. He could make treaties and nominate ambassadors, but only with the advice and consent of the Senate. And, finally, the president could be impeached by the House and tried by the Senate for treason, bribery, and other "high crimes and misdemeanors."

Over the national judiciary, Congress was given several significant powers. First, judges were to be appointed by the president and then approved by the Senate. Second, any judge who violated a code of "good behavior" could be impeached by Congress and removed from office in a manner similar to the impeachment of a president.

But more important, the Constitution gave Congress the power to determine the size of the Supreme Court and other federal courts and to alter their sizes if it saw fit. Furthermore, the Constitution gave the Supreme Court "original jurisdiction" only in cases "affecting ambassadors, other public ministers and consuls, and those in which a state shall be a party."

In all other cases, the Court was to have only "appellate jurisdiction... with such exceptions, and under such regulations as the Congress shall make." This meant that the Congress, by a simple majority vote, could deny the Supreme Court the right to consider certain cases. A Court that Congress considered to have exceeded its authority could be reined in and checked. Congress has rarely exerted this authority, but it is potentially an enormous limitation on judicial power.

Two final ways the Constitution wove the power of the states into that of the nation were through the processes it required before the Constitution could be ratified and amended. Ratification or approval of the Constitution was not to be made by the people of the nation as a whole, but by the states.

"In ratifying the Constitution," Madison said, "each state... is considered as a sovereign body, independent of all others, and only to be bound by its own voluntary acts." Thus, "the new Constitution will, if established," he concluded, "be a *federal*, and not a *national* Constitution" because each of the states will have been intimately involved in its adoption.

Amendment of the Constitution was likewise dependent upon the states. Amendments could be proposed by two-thirds of both houses of Congress or by two-thirds of the state legislatures. But whatever their origin, amendments could become law only after the approval of the legislatures or conventions of three-quarters of the states. Under this rule, Madison pointed out, the states would not only have a say in the ratification of the Constitution, but would continue to play an important role in its development and alteration.

The framers of the Constitution created a government that was "mixed" at two levels. First, the three branches of the national government—the legislative, judicial, and executive—were given powers that checked and balanced one another and prevented the undue growth of any one branch. Second, a system of federalism was established that separated the states from the nation, but joined the powers of both into an interlocking whole.

Under the Constitution, the national government was to guarantee republican forms of government to each of the states and come to their aid in times of "domestic violence." But the national government was likewise supposed to limit itself to its enumerated and listed powers, and respect the rights of the states to independence and freedom in all other matters.

The Constitution has been compared to Newton's theory of gravitation, which was familiar to most of the delegates at the convention in Philadelphia. Newton envisioned a mechanical, clockwork-like universe in which each heavenly body was held in place by and influenced all other heavenly bodies. Order and stability were maintained because the power of gravitation kept each planet and star in its proper orbit and position. The system worked as a whole.

Similarly, the Constitution diffused power among a number of centers—nation, state, the executive, the judiciary, and the Congress. Each had its own, separate orbit of activity. But at the same time each influenced the others and helped keep them in their place, performing their allotted and limited activities.

This elaborate and complex constitutional system, the Founding Fathers believed, was the best guarantee of liberty and freedom for both the states and for American citizens. The checks and balances each part of government had on the others helped restrain what they regarded as humanity's "natural tendency" toward ambition, greed, and corruption. The diffusion of power among a number of centers made it difficult, if not impossible, for one person or group to gain complete control of the government for their own selfish aims.

With the Constitution, the Founding Fathers achieved what had eluded Americans from the time of the New England Confederation through the Albany Plan of Union and the Articles of Confederation. A form of government was founded that combined state and nation and balanced the continued existence of the former with the need for an efficient central government. The Constitution created a new federalism for America, but that federalism was still on paper and had to be worked out in practice.

CHAPTER FIVE

THE TRIUMPH OF FEDERALISM

This Constitution, and the laws of the United States, which shall be made in pursuance thereof; and all treaties made, or which shall be made, under the authority of the United States, shall be the Supreme Law of the land; and the judges in every State shall be bound thereby, any thing in the Constitution or laws of any State to the contrary notwithstanding.

Article VI, Section 2, of the Constitution

On first reading, the Constitution may appear clear and precise. But a second or third closer reading will produce ambiguities in meaning and intention. The document, for example, was clearly intended to establish a national government, yet nowhere is the word *national* used. Moreover, the Constitution makes frequent mention of "states" and the "United States," but offers no exact definition of the relationship between the two levels of government.

These ambiguities, however, were not the result of omission or a failure of imagination, but were intentional. The Founding Fathers could not foresee every problem the new nation would face as it developed. They wanted the Constitution to supply a framework of government in which orderly change was possible and whose details could be filled in later, and then altered, if need be.

They did not spell out, for instance, how far the powers of Congress extended or to what degree the states could pursue their traditional patterns of separateness. Where, for instance, did the taxing power of the national government end and that of the states begin? What happened if the two levels of government came into irreconcilable conflict? Would one have to submit to the other and, if so, who would determine which level should submit and to what extent?

These problems and others would be worked out as they arose. What the ambiguity of the Constitution made possible was two opposing interpretations of its meaning. If it could be regarded as favoring national power, it could also be construed as favoring state power. If it established a nation, it likewise guaranteed the existence of the states.

With the Constitution, the enduring—and unresolved—debate over the nature of American federalism began. And it continues today. On the one side are arrayed those who favor a "liberal" interpretation of the Constitution and support strong national power. On the other are those who defend a "strict" interpretation that would limit national power and give greater authority to the states. But each side has always claimed that it holds the only "true" and "genuine" interpretation of the Constitution.

The Struggle for Ratification
The debate over the nature of American federalism began shortly after the Constitution was completed. In order to become "the supreme law of the land," it had to be ratified by nine of the thirteen states, and ratification was far from certain. The Constitution had many enemies who feared that it would destroy states' rights. In the struggle for ratification, those who supported the Constitution called themselves "Federalists," while those who opposed it were known as "Anti-Federalists."

One common complaint of the Anti-Federalists was that the Constitution would create a government run by the rich and powerful. This fear was voiced by Amos Singletary, a Massachusetts farmer. "These lawyers, and men of learning, and moneyed men" that make up the Federalist Party, he said, "talk so finely, and gloss over matters so smoothly," but they really have but one aim in mind.

And that aim, Singletary concluded, was "to make us poor illiterate people swallow down the pill," while they "get into Congress themselves" and run the country. The rich and well-placed, he warned, not only "expect to be the managers of this Constitution," but also to "get all the power and all the money into their own hands, and then they will swallow up all us little folk."

Other Anti-Federalists wondered if the Constitution could govern a nation as large as the United States. Said George Mason, the author of the Virginia Bill of Rights: "Is it to be supposed that one national government will suit so extensive a country, embracing so many different climates and containing inhabitants so very different in manners, habits and customs?"

"There never was government over a very extensive country," he added, "without destroying the liberties of the people: history . . . supported by the opinions of the best writers, shows us that monarchy may suit a large territory but that popular governments can only exist in small territories."

Another Virginian, Patrick Henry, agreed with Mason and denounced the Constitution as dangerous to American liberty. The president, he claimed, had been given too much power and would enslave the nation. Congress was likewise too strong and would eventually amass to itself rights that now belonged to the states.

But what bothered Henry above all was that the framers of the Constitution had had the audacity to begin its Preamble with the words "We the People..." Who gave them the power to do that, he asked: "The people gave them no power to use their name. That they exceeded their power is perfectly clear." Henry believed that any document that formed a government for the United States should rightfully begin with "We the States..."*

Lastly, the Anti-Federalists wondered how two separate governments, state and nation, could exist side by side. That they would be locked in eternal conflict with one another seemed obvious. Samuel Nason of Massachusetts stated the problem succinctly. "We" in the state government of Massachusetts, he said, "are under an oath: we have sworn that Massachusetts is a sovereign and independent state. How then can we vote for this constitution, that destroys that sovereignty?"

From North to South, the Anti-Federalists called for the defeat of the Constitution—and they were almost successful. Delaware, New Jersey, Maryland, and South Carolina declared for ratification by large margins. But in other states the delegates to the state ratifying conventions were narrowly divided.

In Massachusetts, a change of ten votes out of 355 cast would have spelled defeat for the Constitution. In Pennsylvania, Federalists had to use strong-arm tactics to produce ratification. In Virginia, ratification won by only eighty-nine to seventy-nine.

In New York, the struggle over the Constitution was particularly intense. A majority of delegates at the ratifying convention were Anti-Federalists and it took the brilliant political skills of Alexander Hamilton to overcome this majority. Hamilton ad-

---

* The framers of the Constitution had originally inserted the phrase "We the States..." into the Preamble and followed it with the names of the thirteen states. This, however, proved unwieldy and "We the People..." was used as a replacement. Later supporters of states' rights would use this as proof that the framers had really intended to create a union of states rather than a nation of "one people."

dressed the convention directly, arguing down the complaints of the opposition and pointing out the virtues of the Constitution.

But Hamilton also made use of the talents of James Madison and John Jay. Under the name "Publius," the three men published a series of commentaries that have since been known as *The Federalist*. The commentaries—eighty-five in number—appeared in the New York press and attempted to address every question raised by the Anti-Federalists.

Could the two governments, state and nation, live together comfortably without conflict? Yes, said Hamilton, because the two governments need one another. "A firm Union," he pointed out, will contribute to "the peace and liberty of the States," because it will help them deal with "domestic faction and insurrection."

Will the national government inevitably destroy the governments of the states? This time Hamilton answered no. "The proposed Constitution," he wrote,

> *so far from implying an abolition of the State governments, makes them constituent parts of the national sovereignty, by allowing them a direct representation in the Senate, and leaves in their possession certain exclusive and very important portions of sovereign power. This fully corresponds, in every rational import of the terms, with the idea of a federal government.*

Could the Constitution govern a nation as large and various as the United States? Madison not only believed that it could, he also believed that the Constitution provided the best possible means to govern a large nation. "In the compound republic of America," he wrote, "the power surrendered by the people is first divided between two distinct governments, and then the portion allotted to each subdivided among distinct and separate departments."

This division and subdivision of power, he argued, gives "double security . . . to the rights of the people. The different governments will control each other, at the same time that each will be controlled by itself."

But, Madison continued, the division of power between the states and nation is only one means to limit authority and assure liberty. In a large society like America, "the society itself will be broken into so many parts, interests, and classes of citizens, that the rights of individuals, or of the minority, will be in little danger from interested combinations of the majority." America's very size would be an assurance against tyranny, because the Constitution would guarantee that all of the country's diverse interests and voices would be heard, and in this multiplicity of interests and voices, no one group could dominate and prevail.

No one knows how much the arguments of *The Federalist* contributed to the victory of the Constitution in New York, but ratification carried by a majority of three—thirty to twenty-seven. Ten states had already accepted the Constitution, but the triumph in New York was especially gratifying since it assured that the New England States would not be cut off from the rest of the nation.

Several months later North Carolina and Rhode Island became the twelfth and thirteenth states to ratify. The Federalists had won. Thomas Jefferson was moved by its success. "The example," he wrote, "of changing a constitution by assembling the wise men . . . instead of assembling armies, will be worth as much to the world as the former examples we have given them."

Federalism in Practice

"I will be a peaceable citizen," Patrick Henry said after the defeat of his attempt to stop ratification of the Constitution. "My head, my hand and my heart shall be at liberty to retrieve the loss of liberty, and remove the defects of that system in a constitutional way."

One defect in the Constitution that disturbed the Anti-Federalists deeply was the absence of a Bill of Rights. Another was the lack of any clear statement on states' rights. The Anti-Federalists hoped to remedy these defects in the first session of the new Congress which assembled in New York in 1789.

Indeed, the lack of a Bill of Rights was on the minds of many Americans, and several states had issued statements deploring the lack before they had ratified the Constitution. But the question for Congress was how to provide for a Bill of Rights. Should the Constitution be gone through line by line to remove all threats to individual freedom, as some Anti-Federalists believed? Or could the Constitution be altered by amendment?

Congress decided on the latter course. A Bill of Rights was drawn up which became the first eight amendments. These amendments guaranteed freedom of religion, the press, the right to trial by jury, and the other familiar rights of American citizens by prohibiting the federal government from infringing on these rights. A Ninth Amendment further limited the authority of the federal government. It read: "The enumeration in the Constitution, of certain rights, shall not be construed to deny or disparage others retained by the people."

In the ratifying conventions, six states had suggested an amendment in support of states' rights. The first Congress likewise adopted this suggestion and made it the Tenth Amendment. "The powers not delegated to the United States by the Constitution," it declared, "nor prohibited by it to the States, are reserved to the States respectively, or to the people."

Federalists and Anti-Federalists worked together in Congress to produce the Bill of Rights and the Ninth and Tenth Amendments. But before long, they began to fall out over other important issues. The most significant of these was Hamilton's vision of America's future.

Hamilton was President Washington's secretary of the treasury. But he was also the chief ideologue of the Federalist Party and originated his party's policy. Hamilton wanted an America that was wealthy and prosperous. He hoped to establish a nation in which manufacturing and commercial life thrived.

To create this America, he proposed a host of programs to stimulate trade and encourage manufacturing. The national government, he believed, should have a tariff policy that discouraged the sale of foreign goods in the United States. It should adopt policies that established America's credit on firm ground. He likewise wanted the national government to assume responsibility for the public debt, both federal and state, and to establish a Bank of the United States.

Hamilton's program inevitably encouraged the distrust and wrath of the Anti-Federalists. It aroused charges that the new government was designed to make the rich richer and keep the poor in their place. It likewise aroused their recurring doubts about the powers granted the national government. The Constitution, said William Maclay, an Anti-Federalist senator from Pennsylvania, has proved to be "a vicious trap to ensnare the liberties of the people."

But more ominously, the dispute over Hamilton's program gave rise to sectional controversies. Since the program hoped to encourage manufacturing and trade, the more agricultural parts of the country felt left out. What kind of national policy, the critics asked, benefited the parts of the country where industry or commerce had taken root, but ignored other sections, like the South, where farms and plantations were the primary economic undertaking?

Pierce Butler of South Carolina attacked the Hamilton program from the Senate floor. The national government, he said, was attempting to oppress the people of his home state. Tariffs and duties made goods more expensive for South Carolinians to buy; they were worthwhile for New England, but not for South Carolina. Unless South Carolina were better treated, he concluded, it would withdraw from the United States and dissolve the Union.

Another complaint about the Hamilton program by the Anti-Federalists was that it implied a national government of unlimited growth. The aim of the Federalists, Maclay of Pennsylvania said, was "to overwhelm us with debt" so that "there . . . would be business for the general government with all their train of officers." We will have, he warned, "a Secretary of War with a host of clerks; and above all a Secretary of State . . . and army for fear the Department of War should lack employment." In the end, he concluded, we will be overpowered by the government we have created.

Much of Hamilton's program won approval by Congress. His financial measures helped restore America's credit at home and abroad. Manufacturing and commerce were stimulated. But his victory had been won at a cost. Most of the members of Congress who supported his program were from the North; most of those who opposed it were from the South or elsewhere. Already, the division had begun to grow between those who looked to the nation for programs of improvements and those who feared the extension of national power.

Federalism and the Courts
Another area of growing hostility between the Federalists and Anti-Federalists was the federal judiciary. At the Virginia ratifying convention in 1788 several states'-rights delegates had questioned the power of the Supreme Court under the Constitution. "Would the Court," they asked, "go so far as to call a state before it and render a judgment that would make a mockery of its sovereignty?"

At the time, John Marshall, a pro-Constitution delegate at the convention, assured his fellow delegates that the Court had no such power. "No state," he said, "will be called to the bar of the federal Court." Marshall's assurances helped to persuade several moderate states'-righters to vote to accept the Constitution. Later, as chief justice, Marshall would regret his earlier remarks and call states before the Court in several landmark cases.

Other Federalists were more candid about the role they wanted the Supreme Court to play in the new government. In *The Federalist*, Madison and Hamilton made it clear that the Court was to be a kind of umpire that would settle disputes over the proper sphere of federal activity and the proper sphere of state activities. They also believed that it was the responsibility of the Court to see that there was a uniform system of law throughout the United States.

The dispute over the federal judiciary arose again in 1789 at the first session of the first Congress. The occasion was a Federalist-sponsored Judiciary Act, designed to give strong powers to the federal courts. James Monroe, a representative from Virginia, recognized the importance of the bill when he wrote to Madison that the Judiciary Act "will occasion more difficulty...than any other, as it will form an exposition of the powers of the Government itself, and show in the opinion of those who organized it, how far it can discharge its own functions, or must depend for that purpose on the aid of those of the States."

The most controversial part of the act was Section 25, which empowered the Supreme Court to hear—and therefore reverse—decisions that had been before the courts of the states. The opposition of the Anti-Federalists was profound. Had this provision been part of the original Constitution, they said, the Constitution would never have been ratified. They found it to be another example of a Federalist "conspiracy" to undermine the rights of the states and expand national authority.

But the Judiciary Act passed Congress, pushed through by a dominant and forceful Federalist majority. President Washington added to the Federalist victory by appointing to judgeships, both on the Supreme Court and the lower federal courts, men who shared his nation-centered philosophy of federalism. And because these appointments were for life, that philosophy dominated the courts for more than a quarter-century.

It was not Washington, however, but his successor, John Adams, who appointed the person who, more than any other, came to symbolize the triumph of nation-centered federalism: Chief Justice John Marshall. Marshall came to the Court in 1801 and left in 1835, long enough to leave a permanent mark on American history.

Marshall's Court handed down many decisions, but the following are among the most significant ones that involve federalism and states' rights.

★ **United States *v*. Peters *(1809)*.** This case involved the refusal of Pennsylvania to abide by rulings of federal courts. In 1779* and again in 1803, a decision by the Pennsylvania state courts was reversed by a federal tribunal. The state, however, ignored the reversal and asserted its right as a sovereign and independent government to decide matters for itself.

The question before the Supreme Court was whether a state could be compelled to abide by the decision of a federal court. Marshall came down firmly on the side of the federal courts. The federal government, he wrote, has the power to enforce its laws by the "instrumentality of its own tribunals." Pennsylvania had to obey the reversal.

At first, Pennsylvania attempted to resist the decision by calling out its state militia. But President Madison countered the threat of rebellion by calling up a federal posse of two thousand to enforce the reversal, and the state backed down. The Pennsylvania legislature then issued a statement accusing the Supreme Court of bias against states' rights and calling for the establishment of an "impartial tribunal" to decide matters involving disputes between the state and national governments. The request failed to find much support, either in Washington or the state legislatures.

★ **Martin *v*. Hunter's Lessee *(1816)*.** In this case, the Supreme Court upheld the constitutionality of Section 25 of the Judiciary Act of 1789, which gave the Court the right to review cases from state courts. It was a "doubtful course," wrote Justice Joseph Story for the Court, to argue that the Supreme Court did not have the power to review state decisions because it might abuse that power.

---

* There were no federal courts in 1779 and the reversal of the state decision was handed down by the Committee on Appeals of the Continental Congress. The 1803 decision upholding the reversal involved the same 1779 case.

"From the very nature of things," he continued, "the absolute right of decision, in the last resort, must rest somewhere." And that "somewhere," he concluded, was with the Supreme Court, not the states. Story's decision was so significant that constitutional scholar Charles Warren has called it "the keystone of the whole arch of Federal judicial power."*

★McCulloch *v.* Maryland *(1819)*. The issue at hand was the Bank of the United States (B.U.S.), which was chartered in 1816. The bank competed with state banks in speculation and overextension of credit. In 1818 the B.U.S. called in its loans to avoid an impending economic crash and in the process caused the collapse of several state banks.

Seven states retaliated by passing laws restraining the operation of the B.U.S. within their borders. The Maryland legislature chose to tax the Baltimore branch of the national bank, and B.U.S. officials protested to the Supreme Court that the state did not have that power.

Two questions before the Court were: (1) Did Congress have power to charter a bank and (2) did Maryland have the right to tax the operations of that bank? The case was of prime importance because it was the first time the Court considered the powers of Congress in relation to those of the states.

Marshall decided the first question on what he called the "great principle" of national sovereignty. The national government, he said, was a limited government, but within its sphere of powers it was supreme. In cases where national power conflicted with state power, state power had to give way. The national government was superior, he wrote, because "it is the government of all; it represents all, and acts for all."

The Constitution, he continued, was intended to be a source of power plentiful enough to meet all the "exigencies of the nation." "A government constructed with such ample powers," he went on, "on the due execution of which the happiness and prosperity of the nation so vitally depends, must be entrusted with ample means for their execution."

---

*In *Cohens* v. *Virginia*, supporters of states' rights once again attempted to question the Court's authority to review state-court decisions and once again were defeated. The Constitution, wrote Marshall, created a nation, and that nation is supreme, as are its departments, such as the Supreme Court.

Therefore, Marshall concluded, Congress had the power to establish a Bank of the United States, even though that power was not specifically listed in the Constitution. The bank, he said, was necessary to the efficient functioning of the national government and therefore clearly within the "legitimate" and "appropriate" sphere of congressional action.

On the question of whether the states had the power to tax the bank, Marshall likewise decided against the states. "The Power to tax," he wrote, "involves the power to destroy." And the states, he concluded, "have no power, by taxation or otherwise, to retard, impede, burden, or in any manner control, the operations of the constitutional laws enacted by Congress."*

★**Gibbons v. Ogden (1824).** This case involved state regulation of commerce. The New York legislature granted the Fulton-Livingston steamboat company the exclusive right of steam navigation on New York's rivers. Thomas Gibbons, the owner of a rival company, challenged this monopoly and claimed that it violated the constitutional right of Congress to regulate commerce among the states.

Gibbons lost his case in state courts, but then took it to the Supreme Court. The Court decided in his favor. The power to regulate interstate commerce, Marshall wrote, was granted to Congress for the "general advantage" of the people, and was therefore a "plenary" or complete and full power.

Marshall went on to define commerce broadly. It was not the mere "interchange of commodities," he wrote. Rather, it included "every species of commercial intercourse" carried on between and among the states. This meant that the power of Congress to regulate interstate commerce did not stop at state boundaries but "may be introduced into the interior" of the states.

Marshall likewise gave a broad definition to what the Constitution meant by "regulate." The power to regulate, he said, was "complete in itself." It "may be exercised to its utmost extent" and it "acknowledges no limitations" other than those mentioned by the Constitution. The Congress, Marshall implied, had the

---

* In *Osborn* v. *Bank of the United States* (1824), the Supreme Court declared unconstitutional Ohio laws directed against the B.U.S. Furthermore, the Court said that state officials were *personally* liable for any damages incurred while carrying out a state law that was unconstitutional.

[77]

power to establish commercial unity throughout the nation, and no state had the right to stand in the way of that power.

Through the four decisions discussed here, and others, the Marshall Court reinforced the movement toward national union and a stronger central government. Marshall's contribution to American history was a more clearly defined federalism, with an emphasis on national power. The Constitution, he said, time and time again, had created a nation, and that nation was supreme.

Under Marshall's leadership, writes historian R. Kent Newmyer, "the government of limited authority, so much a part of colonial and revolutionary constitutionalism, became a government of sufficient power"—power *sufficient* to govern an expanding nation, encourage its prosperity, and unleash its great potential.

The Triumph of Federalism

In several of his major decisions Marshall justified his constitutional nationalism as "part of our history," "self-evident," and "universally understood." Nationalism, he declared, was a doctrine on which "the good sense of the public has pronounced" and one that "America has chosen."

Although his statements ignore the strength of states'-rights sentiment in his time, Marshall's judgment was essentially correct. Most Americans did seem to favor some sort of nation-sponsored program of national growth and development, even when they continued to voice fears about the centralization of government.

This was true even of many Jeffersonians. When the Federalist Party lost the elections of 1800, and Anti-Federalists, now called the Jeffersonian Republicans, elected Thomas Jefferson president, there was no great turnabout in American political history, although many observers predicted that there would be.

In his Inaugural Address of 1801, Jefferson favored moderation. "We are all republicans—we are all federalists," he declared.

If there be any among us who wish to dissolve this Union, or to change its republican form, let them stand undisturbed as monuments of the safety with which error of opinion may be tolerated where reason is left free to combat it.

An outspoken critic of Hamilton and Marshall, Jefferson nevertheless exercised presidential authority in a strong and vigorous manner. In 1803 he, along with a Senate majority of twenty-six senators, agreed to the Louisiana Purchase, which more than doubled the size of the United States.

The states were not consulted. The national goverment alone was a party to the contract with France that settled the purchase. Unilaterally the national goverment had acquired a vast new territory from which a number of new states would be created—states that were not part of the United States when the Constitution was adopted.

The Louisiana Purchase thus threatened to undermine the status of the original thirteen states and at the same time added to the powers of the national government. For if the national government could buy land and add new states to the nation at will, where was its power to end? And what did state power mean when the national government, acting on its own, could so drastically alter the relationship between the states and the nation?

Jefferson's states'-rights conscience was stricken by the deal. An amendment to the Constitution was needed to approve the purchase, he told his closest advisers, an amendment accepted by both Houses of Congress and at least three-quarters of the states. Otherwise, he warned, a precedent would be established that would make the powers of the president "boundless."

But Jefferson's advisers believed that no amendment was necessary. The *implied* powers of the president were sufficient, they said, to make the purchase constitutional. And Jefferson agreed, in spite of his professed belief in states' rights and limited national government.

In 1808 the Jefferson administration took another step toward nation-centered federalism when the secretary of the treasury, Albert Gallatin, issued a series of reports that called for a ten-year program of development of transportation and communications—to be undertaken by the national government.

Gallatin's program, writes historian William Appleman Williams, made Hamilton's program look like that of a "fumbling amateur." The coming of the War of 1812 put a stop to talk of internal improvements, but in 1815 Jefferson's successor and disciple, James Madison, once again made nation-supported economic programs a part of his party's agenda for the country.

Madison called for tariff protection of the manufacturing industries and for expanded expenditures for defense. The "General Government," he said, must be responsible for the construction of roads and canals. It was at this time, too, that Madison called for the establishment of a national bank, which was to become the B.U.S., a move the Jeffersonians had always opposed.

It all sounded like Alexander Hamilton. The Jeffersonian party, supposedly the defender of states' rights, had adopted the Federalist vision of a strong, vigorous national government, guiding the country to prosperity and unity. Jeffersonians continued to support states' rights, but their state-centered federalism was now wedded to nationalism and a belief in the importance of national authority.

Perhaps the victory of the Hamiltonians was inevitable. The states'-rights philosophy, after all, is not suited for those who wield national power; it can only restrain them and hold them back. A complete states' righter in charge of the national government is a contradiction in terms.

The Hamiltonian vision, on the other hand, corresponded precisely to the needs of those who exercise national authority. It alone saw national government as a tool for national development and improvement. It alone offered a dynamic ideal capable of guiding a rapidly growing and expanding society.

CHAPTER SIX

THE FATE OF STATES' RIGHTS

It is indispensable that the government of the United States should be restored to its federal character. Nothing short of a perfect restoration, as it came from the hands of its framers. . . . But it cannot be restored to its federal character, without restoring the separate governments of the several states, and the states themselves, to their true position.

John C. Calhoun
A Discourse on the Constitution and Government of the United States

State governments proved as industrious and innovative as the national government during the first century of the Republic, if not more so. State governments were responsible for planning and financing most of the new canals, for the improvement of old roads, and the construction of new ones. They likewise subsidized private commercial ventures, regulated business through the granting of state charters, and undertook numerous other actions designed to encourage or control economic life.

But in spite of these signs of vitality and life, the supporters of states' rights believed that all was not well with the states. The balance of power between nation and state established by the Constitution, they feared, was gradually being undermined by the encroachment of the national government. Soon the states would disappear entirely.

After leaving the presidency, Jefferson retired to his home, which he had named Monticello, but he never ceased attacking Chief Justice Marshall, his distant cousin, and the federal courts. The federal judges, he wrote in his "Autobiography,"

> *are...the corps of sappers and miners, steadily working to undermine the independent rights of the states, and to consolidate all power in the hands of that government in which they have so important a freehold estate.*

"The Constitution," he warned his followers, "is a mere thing of wax in the hands of the judiciary which they may twist and shape into any form they please."

Other Jeffersonians were likewise concerned by what they regarded as the misuse of national power. Some, like John Randolph of Roanoke, a brilliant and eccentric representative from Virginia, broke with Jefferson during his presidency and accused him of forsaking his own principles. Others, like John Taylor of Carolina and John C. Calhoun, wrote books defending state sovereignty and claiming the right of states to secede from the Union if their rights were violated.

But wherever the doctrine of states' rights was advanced, it was most often the philosophy of those *out of power* in the national government. Groups and individuals without access to national power inevitably disapproved of those who exercised that power. The authority of the states was one means at their disposal to counteract the national government and make their grievances heard.

The Kentucky and Virginia Resolutions

The first major declaration of states' rights after the adoption of the Constitution came in the late 1790s. The French Revolution had divided Americans between those who supported the revolution in France—the Jeffersonians—and those who feared its influence, usually the Federalists. Feelings on both sides ran high.

Concerned that French radicalism might upset American stability, a Federalist-dominated Congress passed a series of laws known as the Alien and Sedition Acts. Among other powers, the acts granted the president authority to expel foreigners by executive decree and gave federal courts the right to punish conspiracy.

One section of the Sedition Act declared that any speech or writing against the president or Congress "with the intent to defame" or to bring them "into contempt or disrepute" was a misdemeanor punishable by fine or imprisonment. It was this provision that aroused the ire of the Jeffersonians, particularly after the national government used it to silence several outspoken Anti-Federalists.

Almost immediately, Jefferson and Madison declared their opposition to these laws. The Alien and Sedition Acts, they said, violated the bill of rights that was a part of every state constitution and was therefore an illegal and unwarranted intrusion by the national government into the rights of the states.

"Whensoever," Jefferson wrote, "the general government assumes undelegated powers, its acts are unauthorative, void, and of no force." Furthermore, he added, each state is superior to Congress and had "an equal right to judge for itself" when Congress had exceeded its authority and to decide for itself "the mode and measure of redress." If a state wished to reject an act of

Congress, he concluded, it could do so as an expression of state sovereignty.

Madison took a similar view. "The powers of the federal government," he wrote, result "from the compact to which the states are parties." If the national government, he went on, exceeds its authority in a "deliberate, palpable" manner, "the states" then "have the right, and are duty bound, to interpose" their own authority to arrest "the progress of the evil" the national government has committed.

Jefferson's views were adopted by the Kentucky legislature and published as the Kentucky Resolutions; Madison's were passed by the Virginia legislature as the Virginia Resolutions. Both state legislatures likewise adopted statements urging other states to join them in their protest against the national government.

The request, however, fell on deaf ears. Not one legislature joined Virginia and Kentucky. Some even issued declarations in reply that supported the national government. The idea that a state could nullify a federal law, said a statement approved by the Pennsylvania legislature, was "revolutionary" and "destructive of the purist principles of our state and national compacts."

In 1800 the Federalists lost the presidency and both houses of Congress. The Jeffersonians, now in power, repealed the Alien and Sedition Acts, freed those who had been jailed under their provisions, and returned all fines. The Kentucky and Virginia Resolutions passed into history, to be revived by later states'-rights advocates as arguments in favor of state sovereignty.

The Hartford Convention

The next declaration of the doctrine of states' rights came from the New England states. The immediate cause was the War of 1812. Federalist New England had never supported the war, regarding it as primarily an effort of the South and West, where the Jeffersonians dominated. Making war on England, one prominent New England leader said, was like making war on themselves.

But there were also other grievances. Since 1800 the Jeffersonian Republicans had dominated political life and the Federalist Party had declined. New England felt oppressed by a national government that pursued policies designed to curtail trade with England and France and prevent American involvement in the war that was being waged between those two nations. The curtailment of trade, the chief economic activity of the New England states, had brought economic depression to the region.

The legislatures of Massachusetts, Rhode Island, and Connecticut issued statements deploring the government's policies. That of Massachusetts was particularly virulent and recalled the Kentucky and Virginia Resolutions of fifteen years earlier. "Whenever the national compact is violated," the statement said, "and the citizens of this state are oppressed by cruel and unauthorized Laws, this legislature is bound to interpose its power, and wrest from the oppressor its victim."

Another complaint voiced by New England was the admission of new states to the Union. New Englanders often referred to the new states as "foreign" and resented the power they had in Congress. "This multiplication of new States not parties of the original compact," wrote one New England Federalist, "must soon be regarded as fatal to the rights and liberties of some of the present members" of the United States.

In 1812 Josiah Quincy of Massachusetts warned the House of Representatives that the admission of Louisiana to the Union as a state had dissolved the agreement of the thirteen original states that formed the United States. The other states, he declared, were now free to secede on a friendly basis, or "violently, if they must."

By 1814 feelings against the national government had become so strong that a Boston newspaper could announce that New England would establish "a new form of government," if its interests continued to be ignored. Later in the same year, Caleb Strong, the governor of Massachusetts, sent a secret emissary to London to seek a separate peace for the New England states in the War of 1812, a peace that would leave the rest of the nation to carry on the war with England.*

The talk of secession in New England angered the rest of the nation. In Virginia, the *Richmond Enquirer* called upon the United States Army to occupy the rebellious region and bring it under strict federal control. "No man, no association of men, no state or set of states," the newspaper said, *"has the right* to withdraw from this Union, of its own accord." Unless a majority of the

* In England too there was a call for peace with New England. "New England allied with Old England," said the *London Times* of December 26, 1814, "would form a dignified and manly union well deserving the name of Peace."

states, it concluded, agreed to allow a state to secede, any consideration of secession amounted to treason and should be treated as such.

But New England was not to be stilled. In the autumn of 1814 the Massachusetts legislature called for a meeting of states to air grievances. The meeting should consider what steps were necessary, the resolution declared, "for procuring a convention of Delegates from all the United States, in order to revise the Constitution thereof, and more effectually to secure the support and attachment of the people."

In December 1814 the meeting took place in Hartford, Connecticut. Massachusetts, Rhode Island, and Connecticut attended, along with a small number of delegates from Vermont and New Hampshire. But from the beginning, the Hartford Convention was dominated by moderate Federalists for whom any talk of secession was distasteful.

The final report issued by the convention limited itself to complaints about the commercial policies of the national government and the War of 1812. It suggested seven amendments to the Constitution, including one that would make it more difficult to admit new states to the Union.

But secession was ruled out as a means to deal with the problems at hand. The dissolution of the Union, the report said, should be "the work of peaceable times and deliberate consent," not the result of "precipitate measures" in times of conflict and deep misunderstanding. The more radical proposals of more extreme Federalists were completely discarded.

The South Carolina Nullification Crisis

Economic hard times had stimulated the New England states to call for secession during the War of 1812. Economic hard times also caused cries of secession to arise in the South during the 1820s and 1830s. Since 1819 the price for cotton, the South's most important crop, had fallen steadily, bringing depression. South Carolina was hit especially hard because much of its soil had been depleted by repeated cultivation and could not produce cotton, even for reduced prices.

Southerners, however, tended to blame their economic woes on the policies of the national government. They particularly deplored the tariff. The tariff, a tax on foreign imports, they said, stimulated manufacturing but did nothing for farming. It stimulated American industry—which was almost entirely a Northern undertaking—and ignored the agricultural parts of the nation. Said Thomas Cooper, the president of South Carolina College: "Is it worth our while to continue in this Union of States, where the North demands to be our masters and we are required to be their tributaries?"

This government policy, Southerners pointed out, had created an imbalance in the country. The North grew rich and prosperous, while the South was becoming impoverished. This was unfair, they said, because the national government should pursue policies that benefited all the states equally.

Ignoring the complaints of the South, Congress passed a new tariff law in 1828, harsher than any before. Critics called it the "tariff of abominations." The tariff of abominations caused John C. Calhoun, then vice-president of the United States and a South Carolinian, to write the *South Carolina Exposition*. Since the states had created the federal union in 1787, Calhoun argued in the *Exposition,* they were superior to it and therefore each state had the right to nullify any national law that was hostile to its own interests. The federal government, he wrote, served merely as an *agent* of the sovereign states, an agent that could be dismissed if a state saw fit. *

The South Carolina legislature announced its acceptance of the doctrine of nullification, but Calhoun advised the state to hold that power in reserve—at least for the time being. President Andrew Jackson, who was to take office in 1829, was known to support states' rights and might weaken—or destroy—the hated tariff.

But Jackson proved indifferent to the plight of South Carolina. Over the next four years, the nullification crisis gradually mounted. In January 1830 Senator R. Y. Hayne of South Carolina eloquently defended nullification in Congress. South Carolina, he declared, was free and sovereign—and could leave the Union if it chose. Liberty was a more important possession than Union and to protect its liberty South Carolina would give up Union, he concluded.

---

* Calhoun kept his authorship of the *South Carolina Exposition* secret, because of his position as vice-president. Only later did his views on nullification become publicly known.

But Hayne's speech was answered by an equally eloquent attack on the idea of nullification by Senator Daniel Webster of Massachusetts. "The Constitution," said Webster, "is not the creature of the State government. The very chief end, the main design for which the whole Constitution was framed and adopted was to establish a government that should not . . . depend on State opinion and State discretion."

The Constitution and the national government, Webster went on, were "made for the people; made by the people, and answerable to the people." He denounced as "delusion and folly" the belief that Liberty came first and "Union afterwards." The two were one and the same, he believed. Webster closed with a phrase that entered the memory of the nation and was learned by rote by innumerable nineteenth-century schoolchildren: "Liberty *and* Union, now and forever, one and inseparable."

Later that year, the nullification crisis gave rise to a second significant exchange between national leaders. The occasion was a memorial dinner for Thomas Jefferson on April 13, 1830. The scheduled after-dinner speeches and toasts, arranged by South Carolinians, emphasized the right of nullification.

Both Vice-President Calhoun and President Jackson were at the dinner. After twenty-four toasts, it was Jackson's turn. His views on nullification were not yet known, but in a clear voice, with his face directed toward Calhoun, the President proposed his toast: "Our Union: It must be preserved." Calhoun, visibly shaken, responded: "The Union—next to our liberty, most dear."

In 1832 the crisis came to a head. Congress passed a new tariff bill to replace the tariff of abominations, but the new bill retained sections still objectionable to South Carolina. In November a convention in South Carolina declared the tariffs of 1828 and 1832 unconstitutional and no longer binding on its citizens.

The convention also announced that federal customs officials would be forbidden to enter South Carolina and that any attempt by the national government to coerce the state into obeying the tariffs would be met by immediate secession. The die had been cast.

Jackson responded forcefully. "To say that any State may at pleasure secede from the Union," he said, "is to say that the United States is not a nation." Jackson also believed that nullification meant "insurrection and war" and that the other states had the "right to put it down."

[89]

Congress passed a "Force Bill" that gave the president authority to use federal troops in South Carolina. Angry South Carolinians began to prepare to resist invasion. For a while it seemed as though civil war might break out. But then compromise was reached.

On March 1, 1833, South Carolina agreed to withdraw the threat of nullification. At the same time, the national government agreed to a gradual reduction in the tariff over a period of years. Bloodshed had been averted. "Nullification and secession are for the present," Jackson wrote to a friend, "I think, effectively, and I hope forever put down." But a South Carolinian was of a different opinion. "Nullification," he wrote at the time, "is not dead but sleepeth; the grand object is disunion, and it will be attempted again."

The States'-Rights Doctrine
of John C. Calhoun

Calhoun started out his political career as a nationalist. He served brilliantly in Congress and was vice-president under John Quincy Adams and during the first administration of Andrew Jackson. He was widely respected for his political skills and keen intelligence. Many observers believed that he would one day be president.

But in the 1820s Calhoun lost faith in the national government. He became an ardent supporter of states' rights and a defender of the interests of his home state, South Carolina, and of the South in general. In a series of speeches, articles, and books, many of which were not published until after his death, he developed the most elaborate and complex statement of the states'-rights philosophy ever undertaken.

Calhoun believed that the system of federalism established by the Founding Fathers was no longer working. Owing to the policies of Hamilton and Marshall, the spirit of manufacturing, industry, and commerce now dominated the country. All else was in eclipse. The older, more agrarian America was disappearing.

Against the advance of materialism and greed, Calhoun said, the South had no weapon. The rapid accumulation of capital in the banks and businesses of the North, he pointed out, caused political and economic power to concentrate there. The South was left out in the cold, its plantation system and farms doomed by a national government that ignored agricultural interests.

The Founding Fathers, Calhoun claimed, had intended the Constitution to create a system in which sectional and state interests were balanced and no one majority dominated the political life of the nation. Why had this system failed? Primarily, he believed, because of the development of political parties, an event the Founding Fathers had not anticipated.

Because of the nature of political parties, Calhoun wrote, one party at one time could come to dominate the national government and a majority of state governments. It could control both houses of Congress, the presidency, and the Supreme Court. The policies of that one party would thus become the policies of the nation.

But what could be done to protect the rights of minorities from a majority in power? The ballot box was inadequate, Calhoun said, because it was through the ballot box that parties came to power. Similarly, a free press was no assurance because a majority party, with its access to money and influence, could buy up the newspapers and use them for its own purpose.

The only way to thwart the power of a majority party in control of the national government, Calhoun concluded, was to give the states power sufficient to veto—to nullify—an action of the national government. "Let it never be forgotten," he wrote, "that power can only be opposed by power. . . . On this theory stands our . . . federal system."

The power of the national government should not be allowed to ride roughshod over the states, he continued, because the Constitution granted the states what Calhoun called a "concurrent voice" in governmental affairs. By "concurrent," he meant an *equal* voice, a voice that had to *concur* "in making and executing the laws" of the nation. If the states concurred with national law, then those laws could be effected, but if a state did not concur with a given law, then that law could be declared null and void in the state.

Calhoun envisioned the process of nullification as working in stages. First, a state legislature would call for a convention to consider nullification of a national law. The voters of the state elected delegates to the convention, and the delegates as representatives of a sovereign state would declare the law null and void.

Once the convention had nullified the law then that law would remain inactive in that state unless and until three-quarters of the remaining states should approve of a constitutional amendment that granted the national government the power to enact the law that had been nullified.

If three-quarters of the states approved the law, even then a state had a choice to obey or not to obey. Not to obey, however, meant secession from the Union. Just as the states had "acceded" to the Union through the state conventions that ratified the Constitution, so they could "secede" from the Union in a similar manner, Calhoun maintained, and then become "foreign states."

Calhoun recognized that the power of nullification would hamper the efficiency of the national government. But, he said, the power of nullification was no more than was needed to give a state sufficient power to counteract the national government. Furthermore, he believed that nullification would be used infrequently and only in instances of utmost importance.

But most important, he wrote, the power of nullification restored the states to their proper sphere in the federal system. Just as they had been "the creator" of the system, so they now became its "preserver." Nullification, he concluded, was the "mediating voice"—a "great repairing, healing, and conservative power"—that would remedy the "disorders" of the Constitution and solve conflicts between the states and nation. Nullification, he added, was the only way to assure states' rights and sovereignty against the encroachments of national power.

The Civil War

Calhoun's program reads like an ardent defense of individual liberty and local self-government—with one exception. One "liberty" and "right" Calhoun defended without exception was the right of Southerners to own black slaves. The slave states, he believed, should be assured that slavery would be forever protected from action by the national government.

Many Southerners among the Founding Fathers—like Washington, Jefferson, James Monroe, and George Mason—had deplored slavery and hoped that it would eventually fade away. The effect of slavery on American society was "pernicious," Mason once said. "Every master of slaves is born a petty tyrant. They bring the judgment of Heaven on a country."

But slavery continued and was given a boost at the end of the eighteenth century by the invention of the cotton gin. The gin made profitable the mass production of cotton and tied slavery even more closely to Southern society. Without slaves, Southern whites claimed, cotton and other crops would go unharvested and the economy of the South would collapse.

Between 1800 and the outbreak of the Civil War, however, the problem of slavery grew increasingly troublesome. In the North a deep anti-slavery sentiment began to take root. Many Northerners wanted nothing more than a limitation of slavery to the South and the prevention of its expansion. Others wanted it abolished outright. Southerners reacted to any discussion of slavery with hostility and indignation.

From 1820 on, the problem grew more intense. In Congress, North and South compromised on the admission of new states, allowing one free state to enter the Union for every new slave state. But the compromise did not still the controversy, nor did any other attempts at reconciliation.

Increasingly, the South took refuge in the doctrine of states' rights—and the threat of secession. The Constitution, Southern leaders claimed, gave each state the right to determine its own social and economic institutions. But if the North persisted in its threats to slavery, they added, then the South must go its own way. "The Union of these States is in great peril," Congressman H. W. Hilliard of Alabama told the House of Representatives in 1849. "This Union cannot stand."

Two events brought the dispute to a final conclusion in the late 1850s: the Dred Scott decision by the Supreme Court and the emergence of Abraham Lincoln as a national leader. The case of Dred Scott came first. Scott was a slave in Missouri—a slave state—whose owner had moved to Illinois and then to what is now Minnesota but was then unorganized territory. Both Illinois and the territory were regarded as free areas, where slavery was prohibited.

Scott had moved with his owner and later returned to Missouri with him. In 1846 Scott sued for his freedom, claiming that his residency in free areas had erased his status as slave. The state courts of Missouri rejected his plea, but Scott and his lawyers took the case on to the Supreme Court. By that time, Scott's attempt to gain his freedom had gained nationwide notoriety.

Chief Justice Roger Taney, a Southerner and slaveholder, headed the Court. Four other justices were from the South, giving the South a majority of five out of nine justices. The Southerners hoped to use the case as a means to settle once and for all the question of slavery in the United States. A firm decision, they hoped, would cause the bitter feud between North and South to stop.

The decision, however, divided the nation more than ever when it came down on March 6, 1857. Among other things, it declared (1) that blacks could not be citizens of the United States, (2) that Scott remained a slave despite his residency in free areas, and (3) that Congress had no power to outlaw slavery in the territories.

The North was aghast. Blacks had always been considered citizens in most Northern states. Furthermore, Congress had passed laws regarding slavery in the territories since 1787 and these laws had been accepted by almost everyone. Slavery was now free "to follow the flag," as Northern editorialists pointed out. Congress and the national government could do nothing to halt its expansion; the question had been placed firmly in the hands of the states.

The South accepted the Dred Scott decision as a vindication of states' rights and Calhoun's doctrines of state sovereignty. The North resisted. The New York legislature passed a law which said that any slave setting foot in the state would be immediately free. Everywhere, Northerners regarded the decision as not binding on them. "The remedy is union and action," said the *Chicago Tribune*. "Let the free States be a unit in Congress on the side of freedom." Let the Dred Scott decision be overturned and the election of 1860 "mark an era kindred with that of 1776."

In June 1857 Abraham Lincoln, a lawyer in Springfield, Illinois, announced his opposition to the Court's decision. The Declaration of Independence, he said, had intended to create a society in which all men were created equal, regardless of color. This "standard maxim of a free society," he went on, had been violated by the Dred Scott decision.

On June 17, 1858, Lincoln stated the problem that faced the nation in unforgettable terms. "'A house divided against itself cannot stand,'" he said, quoting the Bible. "I believe this government cannot endure permanently half slave and half free." He continued:

I do not expect the Union to be dissolved—I do not expect the house to fall—but I do expect it will cease to be divided. It will become all one thing, or all the other. Either the opponents of slavery will arrest the further spread of it and place it where the public mind shall rest in the belief that it is in the course of ultimate extinction; or its advocates

*will push it forward until it shall become alike lawful in all
the States, old as well as new, North as well as South.*

Two years later, in 1860, Lincoln was elected president. As news
of his victory reached the South, eleven Southern states began
preparations to leave the Union. They based their right to secede
on the states'-rights doctrine that since the states had preceded
the nation and had created it, they could likewise leave and
dissolve it. By April 1861 the Civil War had begun.

The Civil War was a contest over federalism. It pitted a states'-
rights-conscious South against a North guided by a belief in the
sanctity of the Union and the importance of the national government. To preserve the Union, Lincoln exercised the powers of
the presidency and the national government in unprecedented
form. The defeat of the South spelled the end of earlier notions
of states' rights and independence that had played havoc with
every attempt at union from the New England Confederation to
the Articles of Confederation. The nation was now one and united
and supreme; Calhoun's notions of state sovereignty were dis-
credited. The long, difficult task of creating a nation out of separate and individual states was complete.

II

FEDERALISM IN THE TWENTIETH CENTURY

Our whole life has swung away from the old state
centers and is crystallizing about national centers...
The people move in great throngs to and fro from
state to state and across states; the important news
of each community is read at every breakfast table
throughout the country; the interchange of thought
and sentiment and information is universal; in the
wide range of daily life and activity and interest the
old lines between the states and the old barriers
which kept the states as separate communities are
completely lost from sight. The growth of national
habits in the daily life of a homogenous people
keeps pace with the growth of a national sentiment.

Elihu Root, The United States
secretary of state in an address before the
Pennsylvania Society of New York (1906)

But the truth is that the doctrine [of states' rights]
knows no special habitation. It is a nomad, reviving
whenever and dwelling wherever toes are trod upon or
feelings severely ruffled by the exercise of federal power.

Constitutional scholar Howard McBain
The Living Constitution (1927)

CHAPTER SEVEN

DUAL FEDERALISM

The Constitution, in all its provisions, looks to an indestructible union, composed of indestructible states.

Chief Justice Salmon P. Chase in the case of Texas v. White *(1869)*

After the Civil War, the face of the nation changed rapidly. In 1860 the official census had listed the population as 31.5 million. By 1900 this figure had more than doubled to 76 million. By 1930 there were almost 123 million Americans. The nation of fewer than 4 million that had fought the Revolutionary War and adopted the Constitution had long since ceased to exist.

After the Civil War, too, Americans began moving to the cities. The once-agrarian society of farms and small villages became a nation of large metropolitan areas. In 1890 the "frontier" ceased to exist, meaning that there were no more unsettled areas for Americans to pick up and move to, as they had done in the past. And in 1920 the census revealed that more Americans lived in urban centers than in rural areas.

But one of the most striking changes to come to the nation after the Civil War was the growth of large corporations. Enormously wealthy and powerful, these corporations quickly transformed America into an industrial giant. Often ruthless and always greedy and ambitious, they were a new force in American life, a force that altered state and national governments.

Laissez-faire and Dual Federalism

The dominant American social and political philosophy in this period of rapid expansion and enormous change was *laissez-faire,* a French phrase that can be translated as "let people do what they want." Applied to American political life, *laissez-faire* meant the less intereference by the national government into the lives of individual Americans and the states, the better.

In his *The American Commonwealth* (1888), James Bryce noted the strong appeal the doctrine of *laissez-faire* had for Americans, especially when questions of federal influence over the states arose. The true American, he wrote, can imagine no greater evil than the involvement of the national government in social and economic affairs. Those affairs, it was believed, were best left up to the states, even if the states might err and make mistakes.

What does it matter, Bryce imagined the average American as saying, if the states make mistakes? They "will in time unlearn their bad habits and come out right if we leave them alone: Federal interference, even had we the machinery needed for prosecuting it, would check the natural process by which the better elements in these raw communities are purging away the maladies of youth, and reaching the settled health of manhood."

Bryce's imaginary average American went on:

> *If the people of a State make bad laws, they will suffer for it. They will be the first to suffer. Let them suffer. Suffering, and nothing else, will implant that sense of responsibility which is the first step to reform. Therefore let them stew in their own juice; let them make their bed and lie upon it.*

From his experiences in America, Bryce concluded that for the average American of the 1880s the national government was relatively unimportant because it was still remote and distant from his life and touched "the direct interests of the citizen less" than did the state governments.

An American's attachment to the national government, he wrote, was primarily "sentimental," because he was rarely involved in the workings of the national government unless he voted "at presidential and congressional elections," lodged "a complaint against the post-office," or opened "his trunks for a custom-house officer on the pier at New York when he returns from a tour in Europe."

The average American, Bryce went on, could not conceive that the national government might need more powers than these. After all, the states took care of all essential matters. Why have more government than was necessary? The only direct taxes an American paid, Bryce pointed out, were "paid to officials acting under State laws." Moreover,

> *The State, or a local authority constituted by State statutes, registers his birth, appoints his guardian, pays for his schooling, gives him a share in the estate of his father deceased, licenses him when he enters a trade ... marries him, divorces him, entertains civil actions against him, declares him bankrupt, hangs him for murder. The police that guard his house, the local boards which look after the poor,*

control highways, impose water rates, manage schools—
all these derive their legal powers from the States alone.

Since the states took care of these matters sufficiently, Bryce concluded, the average American simply saw no need for a stronger and more vigorous national government.

In the era after the Civil War, a concept of federalism developed that took the doctrine of *laissez-faire* into consideration. In his book *The Twilight of the Supreme Court* (1934), the great constitutional scholar E. S. Corwin called this new concept of federalism "dual federalism."

Dual federalism was neither nation-centered, nor state-centered, but assumed that each level of government had its own proper duties and responsibilities from which the other was forever barred. It likewise assumed that the Constitution had created two separate centers of power, nation and state, and that each was essentially equal to the other.

"The Constitution, in all its provisions," said a Supreme Court decision of the time, "looks to an indestructible union, composed of indestructible states." The powers reserved to the states by the Tenth Amendment were fixed and certain, and could be changed only by a constitutional amendment. The powers granted to Congress were strictly limited to those listed in Article I, Section 8, of the Constitution.

Over this system of dual federalism, the Supreme Court stood as arbiter, deciding when the national government or the states had exceeded their proper sphere of power and violated the territory of the other. Dual federalism thus sought to preserve states' rights, without reverting to a radical, Calhoun-like interpretation of those rights. It likewise sought to define a national government that was limited, but supreme in its powers.

National Power After the Civil War

In the years immediately after the Civil War, Congress undertook a program of "radical reconstruction"—aimed at rooting the last vestiges of slavery out of the South. In 1865, the Thirteenth Amendment declared that slavery was unlawful in the United States. In 1868 and 1870 the Fourteenth and Fifteenth Amendments negated the Dred Scott decision by making blacks full citizens of the United States and guaranteeing the right of black males to vote.

[103]

These amendments gave Congress the power to see that the laws established by each were carried out in the states. And the amendments specifically denied to the states the right to "make or enforce any law which shall abridge the privileges or immunities of citizens of the United States" or to deny to anyone the right to vote "on account of race, color, or previous condition of servitude," thus throwing the protection of the national government over the newly freed black.

The Fourteenth Amendment also denied to the states the right to "deprive any person of life, liberty, or property, without due process of law" or to "deny to any person within its jurisdiction the equal protection of laws."

Congress sought to put teeth into these laws by passing further legislation. In 1870 and 1871 the Enforcement Acts were directed against states where blacks were prevented from voting. A Ku Klux Klan Act made it a federal offense to conspire to deprive blacks of their equal rights.

And finally, in 1875, Congress passed a Civil Rights Act designed to wipe out social discrimination against blacks. All Americans, the act read, shall have "the full and equal enjoyment of the accommodations, advantages, facilities, and privileges of inns, public conveyances on land or water, theatres, and other places of public amusement." The act likewise assured blacks of their right to serve on juries.

The Thirteenth, Fourteenth, and Fifteenth Amendments and the Civil Rights Act of 1875 granted Congress and the national government significant new powers. Had that power been used, a major social revolution might have been effected that would have brought black Americans fully into American life.

The Supreme Court, however, brought the potential revolution to a halt. In a series of decisions beginning in 1873, the Court declared that Congress had overstepped its authority and intruded into the proper sphere of the states. These decisions narrowly interpreted the Fourteenth and Fifteenth Amendments so that they did not apply to private citizens and destroyed almost entirely the Civil Rights Act of 1875.

★ **United States v. Cruikshank** *(1875).* This case involved an attack by a mob of whites upon blacks attempting to vote. The Court declared that the rights of the blacks had not been violated according to federal law, because the white mob was composed of private citizens, and the federal government had no authority to deal with discrimination by private citizens. Similarly, in the case of *United States* v. *Harris* (1883), the Court said that the federal government could not try whites accused of lynching four blacks because federal law did not protect the blacks from the violent acts. In both *Cruikshank* and *Harris,* the Court concluded that the crimes against the blacks could be dealt with only by state law.

★ **The Civil Rights Cases** *(1883).* In these decisions, the Court found most of the Civil Rights Act of 1875 unconstitutional. It was not the business of Congress or the national government, Justice Joseph Bradley wrote, to involve itself in "every act of discrimination which a person may see fit to make as to the guests he will entertain, or as to the people he will take into his coach or cab or car, or admit to his concert or theatre, or deal with in other matters of intercourse or business."

These decisions, and others, removed from the national government powers that Congress had sought to grant it after the Civil War. By the end of the century, the Court had limited the authority of the national government even further. In the case of *Plessy* v. *Ferguson* (1896), the Court upheld the right of the states to establish "separate" facilities for blacks, as long as those facilities were judged to be "equal" to those provided for whites.

The object of the Fourteenth Amendment, the Court declared, was only to give blacks "absolute equality . . . before the law." "But in the nature of things," the Court went on, "it could not have been intended to abolish distinctions based upon color, or to enforce social as distinguished from political equality, or a commingling of the two races upon terms unsatisfactory to either."

The *Plessy* decision wrote racial segregation—the doctrine of "separate, but equal"—into the law of the land. It forced the blacks—as the other decisions discussed above had done—to rely on the states for their rights as citizens, and not the federal government. And in state governments, blacks found few allies. In the South, the border states, and elsewhere, blacks remained "second-class citizens," out of the mainstream of American life.

**The States in the
Age of *Laissez-faire***
But if most states failed to respond to the needs of blacks, they nevertheless responded creatively to other problems of the time.

One of these problems was the abuse and misuse of power by the large and growing corporations. The corporations overcharged their customers, cheated their own investors, bought the favors of politicians, and committed a host of other acts that called out for reform.

As early as 1869 the state of Massachusetts established a rail-road regulatory commission, empowered to investigate charges of abuse and corruption against railroad companies. In spite of strong—and well-financed—opposition by the companies, four-teen other states had established similar commissions by 1880.

But the strongest drive for reform and regulation of the corporations came toward the end of the nineteenth century, from the Progressive Movement, which began in the Middle West and spread across the country. Angered by widespread corruption in city and state governments, the Progressives demanded reforms. Concerned about the effect the rapid growth of industry was having on American society, they called for laws to protect workers from exploitation. In both areas, the Progressives met with many successes.

The administration of Progressive Republican Robert La Follette, governor of Wisconsin, led to the establishment in 1907 of a Railroad Commission that soon expanded its activities to include the regulation of other public utilities. "The object of our legislation," said La Follette, was not to destroy the corporations, but "to treat them exactly the same as other people are treated." And to make sure, he added, that the vast sums of money at their disposal were not used to corrupt state officials.

The Progressives also won other battles. Between 1902 and 1909, forty-three states passed laws limiting or outlawing child labor. Laws were also passed protecting adult women and men from undue hardship and long hours in factories. Between 1909 and 1920 all but five states established accident-insurance plans that benefited the victims of on-the-job accidents.

The states, under the influence of Progressivism, were also the first to extend the vote to women. By 1898 women had full suffrage rights in Wyoming, Utah, and Idaho, and could vote in certain elections in other states. In addition, state legislatures passed laws establishing public agencies to aid working mothers and to assist dependent children in their own homes, rather than moving them to special institutions. In 1914 Arizona became the first state to grant home relief to the elderly poor.

Much of the state legislation remained on the books, but much of it, too, was declared unconstitutional by the Supreme Court. The Court had knocked down federal civil-rights laws because they intruded into the powers it believed had been reserved to the states. It also knocked down state legislation involving the regulation of industry because that regulation violated private contracts that had been made between laborers and management.

The case of *Lochner* v. *New York* (1905) was characteristic. At issue was a New York law that limited the number of hours bakers could work, since their work was long and exhausting. The Court held that the state law was unconstitutional. Bakers, the Court declared, were of sufficient intelligence "to make their own labor contracts in their own interest." The police powers of the state, therefore, were unnecessary to protect them from long hours of work. If a baker disliked his job, he could move to another.

Three years later, however, in 1908, the Court upheld an Oregon law limiting women to a workday of ten hours in the case of *Muller* v. *Oregon.* The change of mind resulted from a 112-page brief submitted to the Court by lawyer Louis Brandeis, citing medical, sociological, and other authorities who claimed that longer hours would prove detrimental to women's health. But after 1923 the Court returned to its policy of knocking down state laws limiting work hours.

Tendencies Toward Centralization
Lord Bryce was correct. There was a strong *laissez-faire* attitude shared by most Americans in the years after the Civil War. But that was not the whole story. From the 1880s on, there were growing public demands for stronger action by the national government to deal with social and economic problems.

Many of these demands arose because state attempts to control the great corporations proved inadequate. Time and time again, the corporations were able to ignore, circumvent, tone down, or render ineffective restrictive laws passed by state legislatures. Moreover, many state legislators were simply too timid to take on the large business interests of the nations—or had already sold their votes and support to those interests.

As the power—and misdeeds—of the corporations grew, however, public interest in regulation likewise grew. In January 1886 a Senate committee headed by Shelby Cullom (Republican,

Illinois) concluded that "Upon no public question are the people so unanimous as upon the proposition that Congress should undertake in some way the regulation of interstate commerce," particularly as it related to the railroads.

Later that year, the need for congressional action was given further impetus by the Supreme Court. In the *Wabash* case, the Court knocked down an Illinois law that set rates on railroad traffic. The states, the Court concluded, could not set regulations on goods that entered from or were bound for other states—that power, specifically listed in the Constitution, belonged solely to Congress.

In 1887 Congress made use of that power to pass the Interstate Commerce Act. This act outlawed several abuses that were common practice by the railroads and set up the Interstate Commerce Commission to see that these restrictions were carried out. Three years later, Congress passed the Sherman Anti-Trust Act, which placed further limits on the large corporations.

One way the corporations responded to the threat of national regulation was by reviving the doctrine of states' rights. It was a hypocritical move. The corporations had no genuine interest in local self-government or state power. They wanted only to limit the power of Congress to interfere in corporate activities. Forty-odd relatively small and weak state governments were easier to control and dominate; only the national government had sufficient power and reach to hinder the corporations.

But corporate support for states' rights continued into the 1930s. In 1907 Senator Albert Beveridge noted that every corporation with nationwide interests was a vigorous champion of states' rights. And in 1926 William Gibbs McAdoo, who had served as Woodrow Wilson's secretary of the treasury, asked with some amazement how a doctrine that had once been used by Thomas Jefferson to protect the people from tyranny could now be used by monopolies to defend themselves from national regulations adopted in the public interest.

The drive for a stronger national government, however, continued to grow. Between 1901 and 1909 the strongly nationalist administration of Theodore Roosevelt sponsored federal legislation in the area of conservation and supported further regulation of big business. The need for national regulation, said Roosevelt, "is not a question of hair-splitting legal technicalities," nor "of state against nation. It is really a question of special corporate interests against the popular interests of the people."

"It's a comical fact," he continued, "that the most zealous upholders of states' rights are big businessmen," who will profit from weak state regulations. "The most effective weapon" against corporations, he concluded, "is federal laws and the federal executive. That is why I so strongly oppose the demand to turn these matters over to the States."

In 1913 nation-centered federalism was given another enormous boost by the adoption of the Sixteenth Amendment,* which gave Congress the power "to lay and collect" a tax on the incomes of American citizens. The federal income tax opened a vast new source of revenue to the national government. Previously, the national treasury had gathered most of its monies from taxes on imports, liquor, and tobacco.

The income tax, writes conservative Raymond Moley, author of *How to Keep Our Liberty* (1952), "marked the beginning of a rapid rise of federal authority and the decline of state and local importance." It took money away from the states, he notes, that might have been used for local advantage. But more significantly, he concludes, it gave the federal government a source of almost unlimited income that could be used to finance any undertaking it might choose to pursue.

The administration of Woodrow Wilson (1913–21) continued the nation-centered policies of Theodore Roosevelt and expanded them, especially in the area of financial reform. During Wilson's presidency a Federal Reserve Act was passed to regulate money and banking, a Federal Farm Loan Act helped improve the access of farmers to needed loans, and a Federal Trade Commission Act undertook the regulation of trade.

Wilson also presided over the expansion of the powers of the national government to deal with World War I, which America entered in 1917. Wilson's view of the role of the federal government in the American system was a creative one. The Constitution, he once wrote, is a "vehicle of life" whose spirit "is always the spirit of the age."

Wilson believed the Constitution could be interpreted anew to meet new problems and demands. He likewise believed that the

---

*In 1913 the Seventeenth Amendment was likewise adopted, creating a minor alteration in the federalist system. The right to select senators was taken away from the state legislatures and turned over to the people, through general election. Since most states had already taken measures to give the people a voice in the selection of senators, the amendment only recognized what had already taken place.

federalist system could be restructured to meet those problems and demands. But the final responsibility, he concluded, for innovation in American affairs rested with the national government. "For with the federal" government, he said, "lie the highest powers of originative legal determination, the ultimate authority to warrant change and sanction jurisdiction."

Wilson's vision of a dynamic, creative federal government was not completely new. It recalled the Hamiltonian vision of a strong central government that fostered prosperity and promoted the general welfare. Wilson denied that federal regulation and intervention were necessarily bad things. Under him, the stage was set for the vast expansion of federal power in the administration of Franklin Roosevelt.

But not entirely. After Wilson's presidency there was a return to more traditional attitudes toward the role of the national government in American life. Washington reined in its powers. *Laissez-faire* notions once again dominated American thinking. The country grew more prosperous than ever. But in the distance a crisis loomed, and that crisis was the Great Depression.

CHAPTER EIGHT

THE GROWTH OF BIG GOVERNMENT

This nation asks for action and action now. Our greatest primary task is to put people to work.... It can be accomplished in part by direct recruiting by the Government itself, treating the task as we would treat the emergency of war.

Action in this image and to this end is feasible under the form of government which we have inherited from our ancestors. Our Constitution is so simple and practical that it is possible always to meet extraordinary needs by changes in emphasis and arrangement without loss of essential form ....I am prepared under my constitutional duty to recommend the measures that a stricken nation in the midst of a stricken world may require.

From the First Inaugural Address of President Franklin Roosevelt March 4, 1933

When he became president of the United States on March 4, 1929, Herbert Hoover told the crowd assembled in front of the Capitol for his inauguration that "If we survey the situation of our Nation at home and abroad, we find many satisfactions." America, he said was "a land rich in resources" and "filled with millions of happy homes."

"Ours," he went on, is a country "blessed with comfort and opportunity." "In no nation," he concluded, "are the institutions of progress more advanced" and "in no nation are the fruits of accomplishment more secure."

The security Hoover spoke of was short-lived. In less than eight months after his inauguration, on October 29, 1929, the stock market collapsed. It was "the most disastrous trading day in the stock market's history," said the *New York Times*. In a short amount of time, great fortunes were washed away and the economic vitality that had characterized the 1920s disappeared.

It took longer for the full effect of the Great Depression to hit the nation. By 1932, however, between twelve and fifteen million Americans were out of work—or one out of every four in the work force. Innumerable small businesses had gone bankrupt and the banks were about to close their doors. Those Americans who still held their jobs often faced drastic reductions in income, and the savings of many had been wiped out.

But the Great Depression was more than an economic catastrophe. As time passed and recovery did not come, it also became a crisis in spirit. It challenged the long-held belief that given sufficient freedom, the average American could take care of his own needs, without help from the federal government. It likewise caused many Americans to abandon the belief that big government was necessarily a bad thing to be avoided.

The States and the Nation Respond
Several states attempted to develop programs to help the needy and unemployed. New Hampshire, for instance, set up a "job-

sharing" plan in which jobs still in existence were divided among two or more workers. Wisconsin governor Robert La Follette began programs of unemployment relief. In Oklahoma, Governor "Alfalfa Bill" Murray set up relief stations to feed the hungry and ordered policemen not to arrest the unemployed as vagrants.

Other states responded with other programs. But the most successful was New York, where Governor Franklin Roosevelt put into action a new state relief agency, an extension of workman's compensation, and increased state expenditures in public works and highway building. He also tried to get a state-run old-age pension program and stronger restrictions on banks.

Roosevelt took advantage of nationwide conferences of governors to recommend action by the states to counter the problems created by the depression, but few states followed his lead. Indeed, most state governments were bewildered and confused. Most governors and legislatures lacked the courage and imagination to act in the crisis, fearing that anything they might do would make things worse.

In some states, governors limited themselves to statements about the virtues of self-help and the need for patience and restraint in times of crisis. In other states nothing happened because governor and legislature were locked in a power struggle over the proper course to take. In Pennsylvania, for example, Governor Gifford Pinchot tried to institute a program of unemployment relief, but was voted down by a hostile state legislature.

That most states failed to respond meaningfully to the depression should not be surprising. State resources were depleted by the collapse of the economy, at a time when welfare and relief were needed on a far larger scale than ever before. Even those states where action was taken—like New York—soon found the problems raised by the depression beyond their capacity to handle.

The national government, too, was at first bewildered by the depression. President Hoover, a moderate Republican, was reluctant to expand the powers of his office. The depression, he at first believed, was an economic problem that would work itself out in time, as other depressions in the past had done.

When Democrats in the House of Representatives proposed a $2 billion relief program, Hoover denounced it as nothing but "pork-barrel" legislation. As the depression deepened, however, even members of Hoover's own party in Congress called for programs of assistance sponsored by the national government.

In 1930 Congress passed—and Hoover approved—a bill

granting the president $700 million for public works. By the end of his administration, in March 1933, Hoover had spent more than $3 billion on public construction that created jobs for workers and put money into a stagnating economy.

In 1932 an additional program, called the Reconstruction Finance Corporation, helped save insurance companies and other organizations that had invested heavily in the securities of the now-near-bankrupt great corporations. No previous administration had taken such extensive steps to revive the private economy. But in spite of the measures, economic stagnation continued and the depression deepened.

A Contest of Philosophies

In the midst of the Great Depression, in 1932, Herbert Hoover ran for reelection. As his opponent, the Democrats chose Franklin Roosevelt, the activist governor of New York. The campaign quickly developed into a contest between markedly different philosophies of government.

Roosevelt was no radical, but he did propose a comprehensive program of reform and recovery to be undertaken by the national government. An enormously talented politician, he toured the country and spoke about the need for vigorous action by the federal government. Perhaps his most memorable speech was at the Commonwealth Club in San Francisco, where he pledged to give the American people a "New Deal."

Roosevelt was vague on the details of his comprehensive program, but he did promise national unemployment relief and other legislation to shore up agriculture and the railroads and to protect consumers and investors. He also promised that he would cut government expenditures and balance the national budget.

Hoover responded to Roosevelt's program by denouncing the evils of big government. The choice between him and Roosevelt, Hoover said, was a clear-cut one that would affect American history for generations to come. The campaign, he claimed, was "a contest between two philosophies of government."

The Democrats, Hoover noted, "are proposing changes and so-called new deals which would destroy the very foundations of our American system." This program, he warned, is dangerous for the American people, because "You cannot extend the mastery of government over the daily life of a people without somewhere making it master of people's souls and thoughts."

But in November 1932 Roosevelt firmly defeated the incumbent president. Roosevelt received 57.6 percent of the vote to Hoover's 39.6 percent. The people had rejected Hoover's warnings and turned toward the program of national recovery promised by Roosevelt.

The New Deal

Roosevelt's program became apparent during his first one hundred days in office. Among the areas in which the national government assumed unprecedented powers were the following:

★ *Banking and Finances*. In this area, the President promised that his New Deal legislation would provide "strict supervision of all banking and credits and investments," so that money would become more secure in value and the nation's finances, both public and private, would be put in order.

★ *Farm Relief*. New Deal legislation provided farmers with access to low-interest loans and mortgage assistance. It likewise attempted a nationwide reorganization of agriculture to put it on a more profitable basis.

★ *Industry and Labor*. The New Deal adopted various programs designed to stimulate business and improve the condition of the worker. It likewise began programs designed to put people back to work, undertook a large program of public works, and turned money over to the states for unemployment relief.

★ *Conservation*. Many of the public-works projects begun under the New Deal involved the improvement of water supplies, national parks and forests, and other areas of environmental concern. Especially important was the Tennessee Valley Authority (TVA) and other similar programs designed to raise the level of life in rural and undeveloped regions of the nation.

Roosevelt's first hundred days were his most innovative. But he later added other programs to his New Deal. One of the most important of these was Social Security, which was intended to provide a source of income to elderly Americans, once they had retired from work.

Roosevelt regarded the national government as a tool that could be used to do the job of restoring economic health and social vitality to America. "The only bulwark of continuing liberty," he once said, "is a government strong enough to protect the interests of the people, and a people strong enough and well enough informed to maintain its sovereign control over its government." The New Deal, he believed, would perform both tasks. It would establish strong government and at the same time restore the strength of the people.

In March 1937, in his Second Inaugural Address, Roosevelt more clearly defined the responsibility of the national government, as he saw it. His administration, he said, had begun to address the problems of unemployment, hunger, and human misery created by the Great Depression. These problems had called out for immediate action, and the New Deal had responded to them.

But Roosevelt went on to say that he now recognized a "deeper need" that government had to address—"the need to find through government the instrument of our united purpose to solve for the individual the ever-rising problems of a complex civilization."

"Repeated attempts at their solution without the aid of government," he said, "had left us baffled and bewildered," but "We refused to leave the problems of our common welfare to be solved by the winds of chance and the hurricanes of disaster." "In this," he concluded, "we Americans were discovering no wholly new truth; we were writing a new chapter in our book of self-government."

The national government, Roosevelt believed, could help bring the blessings of liberty to every American. By offering economic security, it could create a society free from the fear of want. By offering support to those in need, it could free individuals from the scourge of poverty and give them the chance to develop their full potentials.

The New Deal and the States
There can be no doubt that the New Deal concentrated power in the national government at the expense of the states. In 1890 the national government had spent 36.2 percent of the expenditures of all levels of government. The states had spent 55.6 percent. By 1946, according to conservative Raymond Moley, the share of the national government had grown to 85.2 percent and that of the states had shrunk to 7.6 percent. In 1934 the national government's share of taxes was 63 percent of total tax revenues; by 1946 that share had become 91 percent.

But if the powers and significance of the states shrank owing to the policies of the New Deal, the states can also be said to have benefited from those same policies. Roosevelt was no total enemy of states' rights. "There is a tendency," he said while governor of New York, "and to my mind a dangerous tendency, on the part of the national government to encroach, on one excuse or another, more and more upon state supremacy."

And as president, Roosevelt's views did not essentially change. As the historian James T. Patterson has shown in his *The New Deal and the States; Federalism in Transition* (1969), Roosevelt deplored purely nationalistic programs that aimed at minimizing state responsibility and activity. His ideal was to use the federal government to stimulate the states and local governments into action, not to hinder or control them.

Thus many New Deal programs were designed to invite state participation, as well as that of the national government. In some programs, the funds provided by the national government had to be matched by funds coming from state governments before the program could be put into action. In New Deal programs, too, federal officials often sought—and used—the advice of state and local authorities in order to tailor programs to meet local needs.

Indeed, New Deal legislation tended to create no single, uniform program throughout the country. But the programs varied from state to state, depending on the way the states chose to implement them.

During the era of dual federalism, discussed in the previous chapter, state power had been viewed as a check on national power. The New Deal reversed that attitude and made national power a check on state power. The result was a completely new pattern of behavior on the part of the states.

Patterson notes several of these changes in his book. "The governor of 1929," he writes, "had safely ignored unemployment." But once New Deal legislation had urged the states to deal with welfare and other social problems, "the governor of 1939 enjoyed no such luxury." "Economic crisis and federal response," he concludes, "had combined to push the states into a new role which neither prosperity nor conservatism could destroy completely."

New Deal legislation stimulated the states to develop legislative programs of their own. "There has been a continuous decrease of the state powers," said Olin Johnson, the governor of South Carolina, in 1935, "because . . . the states have not used them, and the people wanted government. If a government does not measure up to its responsibility by the exercise of its powers . . . the powers will not be there."

Responding to the example of the federal government, state governments in 1940 taxed and spent more than they had earlier and provided many more benefits to the public. They also responded more quickly to consumer demands for the reduction of public utility rates and to the requests of labor unions.

After the New Deal, the states revamped their administrative systems to deal more effectively and efficiently with the new demands made upon them. In addition, the states adopted new merit systems and improved old ones to judge the work of state personnel and establish a minimum level of performance for state workers.

Thus the legacy of the New Deal was double-edged. It had concentrated vast new powers in the hands of the federal government. But at the same time it had helped to awaken in the states new concepts of the creative potentials of state government.

The Persistence of Big Government

"Big government" has been with us since the time of Roosevelt. In 1932, when Roosevelt took office, there were 600,000 civilian federal employees. By 1940 there were over one million and by 1980 nearly three million. In 1930 the federal government spent a little over $3 billion. By 1950 that had become $42 billion and in 1980 it was over $579 billion.

Part of the reason for the persistence of big government can be explained by the axiom that says that once an institution assumes new powers it rarely gives them up, unless forced to do so, and that these powers will tend to accumulate and increase as time passes.

But the persistence of big government also has been caused by the continual state of crisis the United States has faced since the Great Depression. The Great Depression was followed by World War II, and World War II by the Cold War. Since the 1930s the resources and strengths of big government have been perpetually in demand.

Roosevelt established the example of the strong exercise of federal and presidential authority in time of crisis and his successors in the presidency have followed that example. Harry Truman (1945–53) offered the nation a "Fair Deal" that expanded the social programs of Roosevelt's New Deal. President Truman also began the arms buildup to meet the Cold War and undertook the reconstruction of Europe after World War II.

President Eisenhower, while often lamenting the decline of the states, nevertheless presided over a national government that was larger and more extensive when he left office than when he came to power. His successor, John Kennedy, committed the United States to an enormously expensive program of space research and development that could only have been undertaken by the federal government.

But the greatest expansion of federal activity after Roosevelt came during the administration of Lyndon Johnson (1963–69). Johnson, an admirer of Roosevelt, called his program for America the "Great Society" and said that it was designed "to complete the New Deal."

Johnson sought—and received—federal programs guaranteeing medical aid to the poor and needy and the elderly. He expanded government support for the arts and sciences. Public and private schools from kindergartens to universities received government funds for expansion and improvement of educational facilities. Low-interest loans were made available to college students as never before.

Johnson expanded earlier federal programs and added new ones. During his presidency, the liberal ideal of the welfare state, in which government supplied economic security to all citizens from "cradle to grave"—came close to realization. Johnson's conservative successors—Richard Nixon (1969–74) and Gerald Ford (1974–77)—expressed concern about the dangers of big government, but were unable to halt its growth.

The growth of big government since Roosevelt can be represented by the steady increase in the number—and size—of the major departments of the federal government. In 1947 the former Departments of War and Navy were combined to create the Department of Defense with an enormous peacetime budget. In 1953, under Eisenhower, a Department of Health, Education and Welfare was created that by the 1970s was spending a larger share of the federal budget than any other department.

During Johnson's presidency a Department of Housing and Urban Development was added in 1965 and a Department of Transportation in 1966. President Jimmy Carter (1977–81) established a Department of Energy in 1977 and in 1979 split the sprawling Department of Health, Education and Welfare into two separate parts, the Department of Education and the Department of Health and Human Services.

The New Federalisms

By the 1950s the growth of centralized government had caused political scientists to develop new ideas about the nature of American federalism. One of the most interesting of these new concepts was put forth by Martin Grodzins. Grodzins served on the Committee on National Goals, which was created by President Eisenhower to analyze the state of American society and suggest areas for improvement. His ideas appear in the publication of that committee, *Goals for Americans* (1960).

Grodzins was encouraged by the state of American federalism.* He noted that the old adversarial relationship between state and nation, in which the states were expected to check the powers of the federal government, was no longer in operation. This, he believed, was good, because the states and the nation were now free to work in cooperation with one another as partners in the American system.

The states and the nation, Grodzins wrote, are blended together like the lines of color in a "marble cake, characterized by an inseparable mingling of differently colored ingredients." This mingling and blending of state and national functions, he argued, was how the Founding Fathers really meant the federalist system to work.

The Constitution, Grodzins went on, had established many centers of power intended to carry out the many duties and responsibilities of government. That the relationship between the states and nation was to be one of cooperation was obvious, he wrote, because the early American government had assumed the debts of the states, in order to help the states out and ease their responsibilities.

Grodzins found other examples of state and national cooper-

---

* Grodzins' views were expanded and further developed by his student Daniel Eleazar in two interesting books, *The American Partnership* (1962) and *American Federalism: The View from the States* (1966). In the latter book, Eleazar writes: "The 50 American states, located between the powerful federal government and the burgeoning local governments . . . are the keystones of the American governmental arch. This was the case . . . in 1789 and remains true despite the great changes that have taken place in the intervening years."

ation in the nineteenth and twentieth centuries. But he found the healthiest development of cooperation to have come during the New Deal and afterward. Federal power, he maintained, did not destroy state government, but enhanced it. The states, he noted, have tended to use federal grants as a "reenforcement" of their own "existing programs" that were developed at the state and local level.

Strong national government was needed, Grodzins concluded, in order to force "parochial and private interests" to work within the interests of the nation as a whole. Strong national leadership, he added, coupled with vigorous and varied responses from the states, "exhibits the American system at its best."

Grodzins's "cooperative federalism" was taken up and expanded by Nelson Rockefeller, the governor of New York, in a series of lectures in 1962.* Rockefeller called his version of federalism "creative federalism." "Our own federal system," he declared, "provides a unique arena for imaginative and inventive action and leadership, responsive and responsible to the people."

The historic application of the federal idea—reconciling unity and diversity—is probably the supreme American contribution to the struggle of all self-governing peoples to build political structures strong enough to assure freedom and order in their lives.

Rockefeller looked not only to the states and the nation for "creative" responses to the nation's problems, he also wanted to make use of the creative potential of private sources of power such as industry and the academic world.

President Lyndon Johnson took up the notions of cooperative federalism and creative federalism and made them part of his plans for the Great Society. At his 1964 commencement address at the University of Michigan, Johnson noted that "There has been much loose talk about the federal government versus the state governments—as if they were enemies."

They are not enemies, he went on, but "separate agencies, each with special resources, each with special capabilities, but both joined in a united attack on the common problems of our country." And since they are separate agencies, he said, each has

*Rockefeller's lectures were published as *The Future of Federalism* (1964).

different jobs to do. The question before the country, he concluded, is to decide which level of government can best perform a certain task, and then to assign that task to that level of government.

Johnson claimed that the "White House has not the slightest interest" in directing and controlling the development of the Great Society. Rather, "we live in the belief that our federal government exists not to grow larger itself, but to encourage the people to grow larger." Furthermore, he added, we believe that "the federal government does not exist to subordinate the sovereign states. We exist to support them."

In 1966 Johnson issued an executive memorandum that carried out these beliefs. "Our objective is to make certain that vital new federal assistance programs are made workable at the point of impact," the memorandum read, and it instructed the directors of federal programs to discuss and arrange all programs with state and local leaders.

After he took office in 1969, President Richard Nixon continued this practice. In an executive memorandum of his own, Nixon called on federal employees to be "more sensitive, receptive and responsive" to the views and wishes of state and local officials.

The Nixon administration also undertook a program of revenue-sharing designed to turn federal funds directly over to state use. The purpose of the program, the president said, was "to reverse the flow of power and resources from the states and communities to Washington and start power and resources flowing back from Washington to the states and communities and, more important, to the people all over America." By strengthening state government directly, he added, "we can make government more creative in more places."

Government by Judiciary

Between 1933 and 1937 one of the most powerful opponents of Roosevelt's policies and the expansion of federal powers was the Supreme Court. In case after case, the Court declared New Deal programs unconstitutional and beyond the power of Congress to enact. The Court favored limited government and a strict and narrow interpretation of the powers granted to Congress by the Constitution.

After 1937, however, the philosophy of the Court began to change. New justices, appointed by President Roosevelt, began to replace older ones. Two of the most important were Hugo Black, a former Democratic senator from Alabama, and William O. Douglas, who had headed the Securities and Exchange Commission.

Both Black and Douglas were admirers of Roosevelt and had worked on New Deal legislation and its implementation. They also favored the use of federal power to bring social justice and equality to all Americans.

Under their influence and that of other new justices, the Court began to interpret the Constitution more broadly. Congress was allowed more room in which to act—without fear that its legislation would be knocked down by a hostile Court. But more significantly, the Court began to declare unconstitutional state laws that conflicted with national law and the Bill of Rights.

Earlier, the Supreme Court had attempted to separate national law from state law and to preserve state legal systems and practices from intrusion by the federal judiciary. The result was a differing—and uneven—administration of justice among the various states. Now, the Court saw as its responsibility the establishment of a consistent and even-handed application of law throughout the United States.

Between 1937 and 1953 the Court began a slow and cautious transition to a philosophy of "judicial activism," or the use of judicial power to enforce change in society. After 1953, however, under Chief Justice Earl Warren, the Court revolutionized American life. In a series of landmark cases the Court overturned state laws and placed new requirements of social justice and behavior on state governments.

★**Brown *v*. Board of Education** *(1954)*. In this case the Supreme Court declared segregation of races in public schools to be unconstitutional. The following year, the Court ordered the states to begin integration of schools with "all deliberate speed." Subsequent decisions knocked down segregation in public transportation and accommodations, in housing, and in many other aspects of American life.

★**Baker *v*. Carr** *(1962)*. In this case the Court ordered the states to reorganize voting districts so that every citizen was granted an equal voice in state government. A subsequent decision ordered reorganization of voting districts for members of the House of

Representatives on the same basis. The result, noted the *Washington Post*, was "a massive change in the nation's political structure" as the states struggled to redistrict according to new population patterns. Many rural areas lost political power they once had, while urban areas gained.

★ *The* **Mapp** *(1961),* **Gideon** *(1963), and* **Miranda** *(1966) Cases.* In these cases the Court established national guidelines for the handling of accused criminals that had to be followed in all states. These guidelines protected the accused criminal's right to remain silent and to have a lawyer.

★ *The* **Engel** *(1962) and* **Schempp** *(1963) Cases.* In these two cases the Court declared that school prayer and Bible reading were unconstitutional. Such devotions, it said, when carried on in public schools supported by government funds, amounted to state support of religion, which was unconstitutional under the First Amendment.

Even after Chief Justice Warren left the Court, the practice of "judicial activism" continued. Under Chief Justice Warren Burger, the Court has knocked down state laws on abortion and the death penalty, and has required the states and localities to provide school busing in order to achieve racial integration.

These decisions by the Warren and Burger Courts have aroused widespread hostility. The *Brown* decision caused many Southerners to revive earlier notions of states' rights and to call for organized resistance to integration. In many areas, the school prayer and Bible-reading decisions have been ignored by public schools which continue these devotional practices.

At one time or another, all the decisions have been deplored by supporters of states' rights and others who see them as an unwarranted intrusion by the federal judiciary into matters that should be settled by the states and localities. What we now have, say the critics, is "government by judiciary."

Government by judiciary is wrong, they claim, because in the American system only Congress and the state legislatures can *make* laws. The duty of the judiciary is simply to interpret those laws. The Supreme Court, they add, should not be in the business of imposing its own views on the rest of the nation.

Critics of the federal judiciary have called for constitutional amendments to deny the Court authority to deal with problems such as abortion and school busing. They have also asked Congress to pass laws that would limit the Court's right to pass judgment on the same issues. They see the "judicial activism" of the Warren and Burger Courts as one more example of the federalist system gone awry in favor of the federal government, and hope to find some means to restore what they believe to be the proper balance between the states and nation.

CHAPTER NINE

REAGAN'S FEDERALISM

We are attempting to improve the federal system so that government can meet the needs of today instead of deepening the mistakes of the past....Those who still advocate far-removed federal solutions are dinosaurs, mindlessly carrying on as they always have, unaware that times have changed.

*President Ronald Reagan
in a speech to television reporters and
executives on February 7, 1982*

The rapid growth of centralized power and the enormous influence the Supreme Court has exerted over American life since the 1930s have led many political observers to speak of a crisis in federalism. The traditional balance of power between the nation and the states, they say, has shifted dangerously toward the nation. Some commentators, like Roscoe Drummond, a Washington correspondent, have even concluded that federalism is all but dead as a vital principle of American government.

Two of the most potent critics of the state of American federalism have been Raymond Moley and John Marshall Harlan. Moley was one of the architects of the New Deal in the 1930s, but turned against the Roosevelt tradition in the 1940s. Harlan served as an associate justice on the Supreme Court for sixteen years following his appointment by President Eisenhower.

For Moley, the idea that the national government should serve as a stimulant to state activity was nonsense. Federally sponsored programs were the wrong way to deal with social and economic problems, he believed, because they inevitably sapped the will and ability of the states to take care of their own needs in their own way. As Washington increases its power, he wrote, the states will become less "competent" and will eventually "wither from lack of nourishment."

"This trend," Moley said, "... will ultimately erase local self-government and reduce the states to the status of mere agents or provinces of the federal government." The federal government, he noted, has assumed many functions that once belonged to the states: assistance to the aged and unfortunate, highway building, the regulation of business and labor, the control of elections and primaries, the enforcement of criminal law, and others. If the federal government has assumed a role in these areas, he asked, what is to stop it from taking over all the functions of state government?

Moley believed the Constitution looked upon the states as protectors and defenders of individual liberty. The gradual decline of state power since the New Deal, he argued, has meant that a "formidable barrier" between the individual and an all-powerful central government has been erased. The development of centralized power in America, Moley concluded, has brought the nation one giant step closer to tyranny and dictatorship.

Like Moley, John Marshall Harlan believed that the federalist system was worth preserving. Federalism and the separation of powers, he said in a 1963 speech at the American Bar Center in Chicago, "lie at the root of our constitutional system." The Founding Fathers, he went on, "staked their faith that liberty would prosper in the new nation . . . primarily upon . . . the kind of government the Union was to have" and not "upon declarations of human rights."

Harlan feared that the Supreme Court had gone a long way toward destroying the traditional balance of federalism. In many of the landmark decisions of the Warren Court, he issued vigorous dissents. When the Court ordered the states to reapportion voting districts, Harlan called it "an experiment in venturesome constitutionalism" and a "radical alteration in the relationship between the states and the Federal Government."

Harlan believed that a true regard for federalism should mean that America was free for diversity and that every state was at liberty to develop its own system of law. He dissented in the cases in which the Court imposed a uniform code on the states for handling accused criminals. "The very essence of American federalism," he wrote, was "that the States should have the widest latitude in the administration of their own system of criminal justice."

It is the "prerogative of the states to differ on their ideas of morality," he added. "The Court is taking a real risk with society's welfare in imposing its new regime on the country." What must be preserved, he concluded, was "a proper balance between state and federal responsibility in the administration of criminal justice."

But what bothered Harlan most deeply about the Supreme Court was that it had "forgotten the sense of judicial restraint." "The Constitution is not a panacea for every blot on the public welfare," he once said, "nor should this Court, ordained as a judicial body, be thought of as a general haven for reform movements." Harlan wanted the Court to limit itself to the interpretation of law and to avoid trying to remedy the "deficiencies in society."

Reagan's Federalism

Like Moley and Harlan, Ronald Reagan believes that there is a crisis in the federalist system. From the time he first actively entered national political life, in the 1964 presidential campaign of conservative Barry Goldwater, he has spoken out on what he regards as the evils of big government. A summary of his political views—as they have appeared in his frequent speeches—appears in his book, *Where's the Rest of Me?* (1981).*

For Reagan, big government is dangerous because it is enormously wasteful and a threat to individual liberty. It destroys self-initiative and creates passive citizens unable to care for themselves. Quoting the ancient Greek writer Plutarch on the dangers of government largesse, he warns: "'The real destroyer of the liberties of the people is he who spreads among them bounties, donations, and benefits.'"

Centralized government, Reagan points out, "was the very thing the Founding Fathers sought to minimize."

> *They knew you don't control things, you can't control the economy without controlling people. So we have come to a time for choosing. Either we accept the responsibility for our own destiny, or we abandon the American Revolution and confess that an intellectual belief in a far-distant capitol can plan our lives for us better than we can plan them for ourselves.*

With James Madison—whom he frequently quotes—Reagan believes that in America "we base all our experiments on the capacity of mankind for self-government." But Reagan fears that the national government has set a bad example for the states in recent years. Like the national government, the states have increased spending and expanded the role of government. And like the national government, Reagan says, they have become wasteful, prodigal, and a threat to individual liberty. Thus Reagan concludes that it is time for *less* government at all levels, but particularly at the national level, where the trouble began.

Reagan frequently spoke about the crisis in federalism during

---

*The book was first published in 1965 and is subtitled *The Autobiography of Ronald Reagan*. Richard G. Hubler is listed as co-author.

his 1980 campaign for the presidency, and on April 8, 1981, three months after taking office, he named a "federalism advisory committee" to advise him on steps that could be taken to restore power to the states. To chair the committee, Reagan appointed his close friend the conservative senator Paul Laxalt (Republican, Nevada).

But Reagan's first major proposal on federalism came on January 26, 1982, in his second State of the Union Address. Reminding the nation that his administration had done much in its first year in office to bring government spending under control, he then presented a plan to remove several federally run programs away from the national government and return them to the states.

The president described his program as a "bold stroke" and then told how it would work. First, in 1983 and 1984, the federal government would assume entire control of the Medicaid program and the states would take control of programs involving family welfare, food stamps, and the like.

On January 27, the day following the State of the Union message, the White House issued a list of the programs of which it expected the states to take control. They included 43 different programs, funded under 124 federal grants, and involved the following areas:

Social, health, and nutrition services. A total of eighteen programs would be transferred to the states in this area, including child nutrition, child welfare, adoption assistance, and others.

Transportation. The eleven grants to be transferred to the states in this area included Appalachian highways, urban mass-transit construction, and grants-in-aid for airports.

Community development and facilities. The six programs in this area included water and sewer grants and waste-water-treatment grants.

Education and training. The five programs in this area included vocational rehabilitation and the Comprehensive Education and Training Act (CETA).

Revenue sharing and technical assistance. The two programs in this area included the Occupational Safety and Health Administration (OSHA).

Income assistance. The one program to be transferred to the states in this area was low-income home-energy assistance.

Reagan believed that this vast transfer of federal activity would accomplish three things. First, it would relieve Congress and the federal government of many responsibilities that now absorbed their time and leave them free to devote themselves to other issues. Second, it would help cut down on waste in government, because the programs, the president believed, could be run more efficiently by the states.

And third, it would allow the states and localities themselves to decide what programs they wished to finance and which to eliminate. A significant amount of responsibility for decision-making would have been returned to the states and a new balance of federalism achieved. The drift of power and influence to Washington would be checked.

Pros and Cons

The president's program elicited immediate support from many Americans; it likewise drew criticism from many others. Illinois governor James Thompson, a Republican, called it "a good commonsense proposal" and welcomed the sign that the president was willing to "move halfway" to restore the balance in federalism.

Representative Marjorie Holt (Republican, Maryland) agreed with Reagan that the forty-three programs under consideration should be turned over to the states, which, she said, "will allow for transportation and social services to operate more efficiently." Senator John Warner (Republican, Virginia) promised to urge the program on the citizens of his home state, where, he pointed out, the idea of federalism had been born.

Many critics, however, suggested that the president had proposed the new program simply to divert attention from the real problems that faced the nation—continued recession, high unemployment, and the high budget deficit for the oncoming fiscal year. Senate Budget Committee Chairman Peter Dominici (Republican, Arizona) found the president's federalism proposal interesting, but added, "It can't take the place of fiscal policy issues."

Democrats were more outspoken in their criticism. Senator Thomas Eagleton (Democrat, Missouri) described Reagan's new federalism as "a radical change" that called for "the dismantling of the federal government" and assumed that "everything the federal government has done is evil, incompetent, and self-serving."

Reverend Joseph Lowery, the president of the Southern Christian Leadership Conference, said that Reagan's plan was actually a revival of "the old Confederatism" and urged "black national resistance" to it. The new federalism, he feared, would halt black social progress and harm the blacks' chances for complete equality with other Americans.

Reagan's plan, Lowery said, pays "almost no attention... to a dismal national unemployment rate," but instead, he went on, "offers a radical negative restructuring... of American society... which would mean... leaving critical national concerns to the uncertain mercies of 50 colonies with uneven resources, capabilities, and commitment to equity for the least advantaged."

Dr. John Hanson, executive director of the National Conference on Social Welfare, opposed the new federalism because he feared that the states would not act responsibly in continuing needed programs. "Many citizens in need of services or benefits," he predicted, "will be unable to obtain what they require to be independent or productive." Hanson proposed that all welfare programs remain the responsibility of the federal government.

Problems
Critics of Reagan's New Federalism found three general problems that they believed would prevent the program from working as the president proposed.

★ *How Would the States Pay For It?* Obviously, if the states were to assume responsibility for forty-three new programs, they would have to find a source of revenue to finance those programs. But how was this to be done when the mood of the nation was against tax increases and strongly in favor of tax decreases? Furthermore, where was the money to be found in a time of deep recession and high unemployment?

Reagan's program has a "nice appeal to local home rule and self-determination," said John Vasconcellos, chairman of the California assembly's Ways and Means Committee and a Democrat, "but we are in the red, on the verge of bankruptcy, and there's nothing we could pick up" to pay for the programs.

Harry Steben, a Democratic state legislator from Minnesota,

was of the same mind. "We don't have enough money to live up to the state's responsibility let alone step in where the federal government has pulled out. What we're facing is an anti-government movement, not a pick-up or even a do-as-much-as-you-did-before movement."

Representatives for the states also pointed out that Reagan's plan for financing the trust fund through federal excise taxes and oil taxes would prevent the states from raising taxes in those areas, and thus deny them a source of possible income to finance the programs. And Representative Kent Hance (Democrat, Texas) complained that the president was expecting oil-rich Texas "to subsidize his New Federalism" and "we want none of it."

★*The CBO Estimate and the Trust Fund.* In the spring of 1982 a Congressional Budget Office (CBO) analysis of Reagan's New Federalism program showed that the trust fund proposed by the president was far too small to finance the transfer of the programs to the states. CBO director Alice M. Rivlin estimated that the trust fund was $15. billion short of the needed amount.

Rivlin calculated that $20.6 billion would be added to state costs by assuming control of welfare programs and food stamps, plus $41.4 billion from the other programs—for a total of $62 billion. The trust fund as set up, she said, could supply the states only $47 billion—$15 billion that the states would have to find some way to finance.

★*The Problem with Medicaid.* Many state officials expressed their approval of Reagan's proposal that the federal government assume total control of Medicaid. In recent years, Medicaid had been the most expensive and rapidly growing welfare program—and promised to continue to grow at a fast pace, placing new burdens on state government.

Critics of the new federalism, however, doubted the feasibility of allowing the federal government to assume total control of the program. The problem was the great diversity in the programs now administered by the states. In California, a family of four whose income was under $7,800 was eligible for Medicaid benefits. But in Arkansas, a family of four had to make under $3,100 before it was eligible. California supplied thirty different types of optional medical services above those required by U.S. law, but a state like Alabama supplied only twelve.

If Medicaid were run by the federal government, critics pointed out, equal standards would have to be applied to all the states. This would mean one of two things, they said. Either the standards in states like California would be dropped to bring them into line with states like Arkansas or Alabama, or the low standards of Arkansas and Alabama would be raised, which would mean that Medicaid would become more expensive and will add to the national budget at a time when expenses were being cut back.

Discussion and Compromise
In the weeks that followed the State of the Union message, the president's new federalism program was widely discussed—as Reagan intended it should be. In his speech, he said that his proposal would have little merit unless the full cooperation of state and local officials were forthcoming.

In the first week of February 1982 the National Conference of State Legislatures and the National Governors Association met in Washington, D. C. Reagan promised the assembled leaders of both organizations that he would be flexible on his new federalism proposal and remain open to suggestion. Following the president, White House Intergovernmental Liaison Richard Williamson reiterated the promise of flexibility and said that discussions with state and local leaders would begin soon.

Speaker of the House "Tip" O'Neill (Democrat, Massachusetts) and Senate Majority Leader Howard Baker (Republican, Tennessee) also addressed the conferences. O'Neill attacked the new federalism program and called it "part of the overall retrenchment of social policy" followed by the Reagan administration. He promised that the House of Representatives would carry out a "hard scrutiny" of the program, but likewise promised that the House would "not take federalism and put it under the table." He suggested that the Democrats might propose a new federalism program of their own.

At one point, O'Neill asked the Republican governor of Delaware, Pierre duPont, who was born in 1935 into a wealthy family, if he remembered the Great Depression. If he did remember the depression, he told duPont, then he would know that "local governments couldn't handle the programs" that were needed for the poor and unemployed. "That's why they were turned over to the federal government" in the first place, O'Neill explained.

Senator Baker, on the other hand, described the New Federalism program as offering a "now or never" opportunity to the

[136]

country, and said that he supported it wholeheartedly. He pledged that the Senate would hold hearings on the New Federalism sometime in 1982.

At the governor's conference, moderates and conservatives dominated. The governors turned down proposals to shelve discussion of the New Federalism until the recession was over. Instead, they voted to consider the Reagan plan and issue a response to it sometime later in the year.

Moderates and conservatives likewise dominated the meeting of the state legislators. Liberals attempted to rally support for a proposal by Democratic New York Assemblyman William Passannante that called on the federal government to reduce military spending, restructure the corporate-tax program, and put an end to all cuts in domestic programs. But the proposal failed and the conference issued a resolution calling for serious consideration of the New Federalism.

In the spring and early summer of 1982 discussions continued between the White House and representatives of the governors and the state legislatures. The White House announced that it was willing to finance the New Federalism's trust fund through the income tax, rather than the excise and oil taxes, so that sufficient funds for the transfer of the programs would be forthcoming.

In the spirit of compromise, the White House also offered a second alteration in the program. If the states would be willing to assume total responsibility for income-maintenance programs for the ablebodied poor, it said, then the federal government would finance all welfare-assistance programs for the aged, blind, and severely disabled. Many state governors held back from support of the compromise, however, because they believed, along with Republican Governor Richard Snelling of Vermont, "that income security should be primarily a responsibility of the federal government."

At times, the negotiations seemed to be going badly. On April 8, the *Washington Post* issued an editorial with the title "The Late New Federalism?" "The Administration's 'new federalism' plan," the editorial said, "has entered that embarrassing period when everyone knows that its ailments are terminal but no one wants to pronounce the case hopeless."

"The trouble is aggravated," it continued, "by the suspicions of many governors and mayors that the proposals are motivated not by a concern for the untidiness of the federal system but rather by a desire to unload major parts of the federal budget onto their shoulders."

But in the first week of May, a new compromise was reached, which the press called "Son of New Federalism." Under the revised plan, Washington promised to retain control of the food-stamps program and assume responsibility for most—or perhaps all—of Medicaid. The parts of Medicaid to be controlled by the federal government would be worked out later, when it was decided what level of medical care to grant the entire nation.

The states would take control of most family-welfare programs, but new minimum standards would be required that would raise welfare payments in the states that now had the lowest benefits. The federal trust fund would be used to help those states with high unemployment or low tax capacity. The states were also to take charge of a variety of health, education, urban-aid, and other programs.

The Summer of 1982

In June the Reagan administration began a new initiative for nationwide acceptance of its federalism program. At the annual meeting of the American Legislative Exchange Council in Chattanooga, Tennessee, White House aide Richard Williamson emphasized the importance of the program. "New Federalism," he said, "is out to change the balance of power between the state and local governments and the federal government that has been bent badly out of shape as Washington assumed more power over the lives of every American."

Williamson announced that further discussions would take place at the White House between Reagan, the governors, and state legislators in the following weeks. The final program, he said, would be delivered to the nation by the President in July.

On July 13, 1982, President Reagan traveled by helicopter from Washington to Baltimore, Maryland, where he addressed a convention of the National Association of Counties. He used the occasion to speak of his new federalism. He acknowledged that many changes had been made in the program since he had first proposed it earlier in the year, but hoped that Congress would quickly pass the "new package."

The new package Reagan described called for "federal assumption of Medicaid responsibilities in return for the state take-over of aid to families with dependent children." The Food Stamp Program, the President said, had been "dropped from the swap."

Reagan noted that provisions had been made so that the states and localities would be "guaranteed 100 percent" of the funds needed to finance the takeover of the former federal programs. He also noted that the states would not have the choice to drop the former federal programs until 1985, and could do so then only after consultation "with local elected officials."

The portion of responsibility to be shifted to the states, Reagan said, totaled $22.8 billion out of a federal budget of $777.6 billion. Out of the $22.8 billion, he added, $7.925 billion would involve social, health, and nutrition services, $6.53 billion community development and facilities, $4.442 billion education and training programs, $2.0174 billion transportation programs, and $1.9 billion energy assistance programs.

"Our tax dollars," the President pointed out, "have been filtering through too many hands at too many levels with a little less getting through at each step. Together we can reduce Washington's percentage and get the power and the resources back to the American people. After all, it's their money."

As he had on frequent occasions in the past, President Reagan once again declared that his administration was in an "epic struggle" to restore the govermental balance between the states and the nation intended by the Constitution. He likewise pledged that his administration would restore the Tenth Amendment of the Constitution, which guarantees rights to the states, to its proper place in the American constitutional system.

"We are turning America away from yesterday's policies of big-brother goverment," the President said. "We are determined to restore power and authority to the states and localities, returning as much decision-making as possible to the level of goverment where services are delivered."

"In the recent past," he continued, "as the federal government has pushed each city, county, and state to be more like every other, we have begun to lose one of our greatest strengths: our diversity as a people. We must stop trying to homogenize America."

The president's new package met with criticism from several quarters. Senator David Durenberger (Republican, Minnesota), a member of the president's political party, found the basic notion of a new federalism to be "sound," but believed that several of its provisions were what he called a lot of "baloney."

The new federalism, he said, raises "the big question of this election year. Does this administration—does my party—care about the poor? Is the 'New Federalism' a smoke screen for a repeal of the New Deal? Is 'private-sector initiative' a fig leaf to cover a lack of compassion?" Durenberger's views were important, because he is chairman of the Senate committee that will consider the president's federalism program before it goes to the Senate floor for a vote.

Governor Richard Snelling (Republican, Vermont), chairman of the National Governor's Conference, also believed that the president's new package had problems that needed ironing out. National standards would have to be established for the programs turned over to the states, he believed, so that some states would not lag behind others in carrying out the programs.

Snelling also believed that states deeply stricken by the current recession, like Michigan, would need special help if they were to assume the burden of the new programs. The basic issue involved, he concluded, was "fairness"—and fairness meant that no state or group of people, like the poor, would be hurt by the New Federalism program.

Are the States Up to
the New Federalism?

Many political observers wonder if the states are up to the vast new responsibilities Reagan wants to place upon them. After all, they point out, it was the failure and inability of the states to regulate the corporations of the 1880s and 1890s that led to the federal government's stepping in to supply the needed regulations and restrictions.

Similarly, they continued, it was the failure and inability of the states to handle the problems of the Great Depression that led to the great advance in federal power under Franklin Roosevelt. Can the states handle the complex problems of modern society? Or will they once again prove inadequate and inept in meeting new challenges?

Ross Doyen, president of the Kansas state senate and of the National Conference of State Legislators and a wheat farmer, believes that the states are up to the challange. "One of the most impressive chapters in our recent political history," Doyen wrote in the October 25, 1981, *Washington Post*, "is the resurgence in state government at a time when the federal government has been failing."

Quoting a study by the Eagleton Institute of Rutgers University, Doyen notes that "the people who serve as state legislators are not what they used to be. The new breed is young, well educated, bright, hardworking, aggressive, and sometimes zealous."

"The transformation of the states," he maintains, "began early in the 1970s," and was the result of the Supreme Court's order that state voting districts be reapportioned according to new population patterns. The Supreme Court decision, Doyen says, "opened up state legislatures to a new generation of people" and "those people launched what has been called 'the most extensive wave of state institutional reform in history.'"

Under the new leadership, Doyen claims, the states were able to take the lead in a number of new programs. Among the most important of these new programs he lists are compensation to the victims of crime, containing the cost of health care, no-fault insurance, sunshine laws that opened up the workings of state government for all to see, and state fiscal notes and economic impact statements that make it able to trace the financial implications of proposed legislation.

In the same period, Doyen adds, a majority of the states became the principal source of funding for their public schools and provided more grant funds to the localities than did the federal government. Furthermore, he believes, the states were able to target these funds more effectively and efficiently than Washington.

Doyen adds one cautionary note about the states. By allowing the states more power, he says, we give them the capacity to act responsibly, "but the door will be left open for some to act very irresponsibly." For those states—and he believes they will be few—that fail to pursue "the uniform concept of justice for which this republic was founded," federal intervention might be necessary.

Gregg Easterbrook, on the other hand, has strong doubts about the capacity of the states. Unlike Doyen, he believes that the New Federalism will cause most states to act irresponsibly. An editor of *The Washingtonian* magazine, Easterbrook expressed his views in the January 31, 1982, issue of the *Washington Post* in an article titled "Forget Government Close to the People: For Waste, Fraud and Abuse, Washington Has Nothing on Our States and Cities."

State governments, he notes, are already a "larger and faster-growing organism" than federal government. In the 1970s, he writes, state governments employed 3.5 million workers, while the federal government employed 2.8 million. During the same period, he claims, there were numerous examples of waste and inefficiency on the part of the states, sufficient to prove that they can handle problems no better than the national government.

But Easterbrook sees a deeper danger in the New Federalism. "Our society," he writes, "is undergoing a transition to an information society which is reshaping our nation." "Rather than retrenchment," he continues, "we need a push . . . to provide research and technological literacy—more math, science and computer instruction. . . . We need, in short, a national summons to excellence rather than a wrenching debate about how to redistribute crumbs from a shrinking pie."

Easterbrook fears that most states simply do not have the resources—or the will—to provide the thrust needed to bring America apace with rapidly developing technology. National guidelines are needed, he believes, and a federally sponsored program.

Nationally syndicated columnist David Broder offers another reason to doubt the capacities of the states. In the past, Broder has been a strong advocate of state government, but in his February 17, 1982, column in the *Washington Post*, he pointed out that most states were being "casually laggard" about their duty to reapportion voting districts on the basis of the 1980 census. Only 174 out of 435 members of the House of Representatives, he noted, know what their districts will be for the 1982 election, and most state legislative districts have likewise not been redrawn.

If the states fail to live up to their responsibilities in this area, Broder asks, how can they be expected to handle the transfer of programs under the New Federalism?

The Supreme Court and Federalism
At present there are more than thirty bills before Congress designed to limit the power of the Supreme Court to make decisions in controversial areas such as abortion, school prayer, and busing to achieve racial integration. Supporters of the bills argue that these issues are more properly handled by elected officials in Congress and the states and localities than by judges.

The Reagan administration, however, has chosen a different way to deal with these problems. It, too, has little sympathy with the Court's controversial statements, but believes that they are best dealt with through Constitutional amendment than by tampering with the traditional authority of the Court.

On May 6, 1982, William French Smith, Reagan's attorney general, expressed his serious doubts about any law that would strip the Court of power. "Congress may not," he said, "consistent with the Constitution, make 'exceptions' to Supreme Court jurisdiction which would intrude upon the core functions of the Supreme Court as an independent and equal branch of our system of separation of powers. . . . The integrity of our system of federal law depends upon a single court of last resort having a final say on the resolution of federal questions."

On the same day, President Reagan announced his support for an amendment to the Constitution that would allow public schools to hold prayer services. The amendment would erase the 1962 Supreme Court decision declaring school prayer unconstitutional, but would have to be approved by two-thirds of both houses of Congress and three-quarters of the states. This method of change, the Reagan administration seemed to be saying, was preferable to the questionable step of destroying the Court's power.

The Supreme Court, however, has changed markedly since its era of "judicial activism" under Chief Justice Warren and the early years under Chief Justice Burger. Part of that change has been in the interpretation of the federalist system.

In 1976, for the first time in forty years, the Court made use of the Tenth Amendment's guarantee of state sovereignty to strike down a federal law. In the case *National League of Cities* v. *Usery,* the Court declared that Congress could not require state and local governments to pay their employees according to federal wage-and-hour standards.

Other decisions of the Burger Court have similarly supported states' rights by deferring to state governments and allowing state legislatures more room to innovate and experiment with law. This respect for traditional views on federalism has appeared in decisions written by Justice William Rehnquist, but also has been supported by Chief Justice Burger and others.

Historians have noted that the views of the Supreme Court change to fit the mood of the nation. In the 1930s and afterward, the Court altered its philosophy to fit the New Deal and the trends of the times. Just so, the Burger Court has moved toward a stronger sense of judicial restraint and conservatism that seem to characterize the 1980s.

[143]

EPILOGUE

Enormous differences separate the America of the Founding Fathers from the America of today, yet the debate over the federalist system has remained largely the same. From Alexander Hamilton and Chief Justice Marshall through Lincoln and Franklin Roosevelt, there have been those who support a nation-centered federalism and a strong and vigorous national government. From Jefferson and Thomas Burke and on to President Reagan, others have feared centralized government and looked to the states to counterbalance national authority.

At times in American history, it has seemed that a balance had been struck between state and national power, but that balance has always shifted, and will continue to shift. Future generations will offer new interpretations of the federalist system to replace earlier ones. "Thank God for the limitations inherent in our federal system," wrote Justice Louis Brandeis in the 1920s. "Conflict between federal and state authority means 'vibrations of power,' and this . . . is the 'genius of our government.'"

That Reagan could propose a vast shift of federal powers to the states after fifty years of steady growth by the federal government reveals something of the health and flexibility of American institutions. That the program itself could be developed through discussion and compromise between the White House and the governors and other representatives of the states shows that federalism is still alive.

Will the New Federalism succeed? Senator Mark Hatfield (Republican, Oregon) has said that "success in achieving this remarkable program . . . will ultimately hinge on an economic rebirth in the coming year"—and he is probably correct. If recession continues and unemployment rises, the New Federalism will be scrapped in favor of increased federal programs to meet difficult economic problems.

But in final analysis, the success of any program designed to support state authority rests with the states themselves. This was noted in 1906 by Elihu Root, Theodore Roosevelt's secretary of state:

> *The true and only way to preserve state authority is to be found in the awakened conscience of the states, their broadened views and higher standard of responsibility to the general public; in effective legislation by the states, in conformity to the general moral sense of the country; and in the vigorous exercise for the general public good of that state authority which is to be preserved.*

In short, state governments must prove themselves responsible to the needs of the people as a whole, and not to special interests.

It is doubtful that a wholesale restoration of state power is possible in the twentieth century. Problems that were once local have become national in scope. Americans wherever they live have more interests in common than they had two hundred years ago. But it is possible that the Reagan administration has within its power the ability to reverse the trend toward big government and effect a basic change in American life. "A little rebellion now and then," said Thomas Jefferson over two hundred years ago, is a good thing.

FOR FURTHER READING

A useful textbook on federalism is W. Brooke Graves, *American Intergovernmental Relations: Their Origins, Historical Development, and Current Status* (1964). This book contains excellent bibliographical references at the end of every chapter.

On the origins of federalism and states' rights see Clinton Rossiter, *1787: The Grand Convention* (1966);* A. T. Mason, *The States' Rights Debate* (1964);* and William P. Murphy, *The Triumph of Nationalism: State Sovereignty, the Founding Fathers, and the Making of the Constitution* (1967). *The Federalist*, written by Alexander Hamilton, James Madison, and John Jay, is essential to an understanding of the federalist system and is available in a number of modern editions. There are also modern editions of James Bryce, *The American Commonwealth* (1888).*

The author has mentioned several works in the footnotes of this book; each of these works is recommended. On the development of federalism, the reader should see the very helpful C. Herman Pritchett, *The American Constitutional System* (1981);* *The Federal System in Constitutional Law* (1978), by the same author; W. H. Bennett, *American Theories of Federalism* (1964); Aaron Wildavsky, *American Federalism in Perspective* (1967); and the excellent work by Richard Leach, *American Federalism* (1970).*

On federalism in the 1930s, see James T. Patterson, *The New Deal and States* (1969);* on the controversy surrounding the Supreme Court in recent years, see Stephen Goode, *The Controversial Court* (1982);* and on the states'-rights doctrines of Calhoun, see Richard Current, *John C. Calhoun* (1963).*

*An asterisk denotes books of special interest to younger readers.

[147]

INDEX